INTRODUCTORY MUSICIANSHIP

A Workbook

SIXTH EDITION

Theodore A. Lynn

Los Angeles Valley College

THOMSON
™
SCHIRMER

AUSTRALIA • CANADA • MEXICO • SINGAPORE • SPAIN
UNITED KINGDOM • UNITED STATES

Publisher: Clark G. Baxter
Senior Development Editor: Sharon Adams Poore
Assistant Editor: Julie Iannacchino
Editorial Assistant: Jonathan Katz
Technology Project Manager: Jennifer Ellis
Marketing Manager: Mark Orr
Marketing Assistant: Justine Ferguson
Advertising Project Manager: Brian Chaffee
Project Manager, Editorial Production: Dianne Toop
Print/Media Buyer: Robert King

Permissions Editor: Stephanie Keough-Hedges
Production Service: A-R Editions, Inc.
Text Designer: A-R Editions
Copy Editor: A-R Editions
Cover Design: Andrew Ogus
Cover Image: © Lawrence Lawry/Getty Images/PhotoDisc
Cover Printer: Malloy Lithographing, Inc.
Compositor: A-R Editions
Printer: Malloy Lithographing, Inc.

Printed in the United States of America
2 3 4 5 6 7 06 05 04 03

For more information about our products, contact us at:
Thomson Learning Academic Resource Center
1-800-423-0563
For permission to use material from this text, contact us by:
Phone: 1-800-730-2214   **Fax:** 1-800-730-2215
Web: http://www.thomsonrights.com

Library of Congress Cataloging-in-Publication Data

Lynn, Theodore A.
  Introductory musicianship : a workbook / Theodore A. Lynn.—6th ed.
    p. cm.
  Includes index.
  ISBN 0-15-506097-X
    1. Music theory—Elementary works. I. Title.

MT7 .L97 2003
781—dc21   2002022720

Wadsworth/Thomson Learning
10 Davis Drive
Belmont, CA 94002-3098
USA

Asia
Thomson Learning
5 Shenton Way #01-01
UIC Building
Singapore 068808

Australia
Nelson Thomson Learning
102 Dodds Street
South Melbourne, Victoria 3205
Australia

Canada
Nelson Thomson Learning
1120 Birchmount Road
Toronto, Ontario M1K 5G4
Canada

Europe/Middle East/Africa
Thomson Learning
High Holborn House
50/51 Bedford Row
London WC1R 4LR
United Kingdom

Latin America
Thomson Learning
Seneca, 53
Colonia Polanco
11560 Mexico D.F.
Mexico

Spain
Paraninfo Thomson Learning
Calle/Magallanes, 25
28015 Madrid, Spain

Contents

Piano Keyboard (foldout)

Preface

Introductory Musicianship, now in its sixth edition, is a text-workbook in musical fundamentals that places particular emphasis on the basic skills of reading and writing music. It assumes students have no prior knowledge of music, and it is appropriate in either a one- or two-semester fundamentals course for nonmajors or in an introductory theory course for majors. The unusual organization of the book—six text units with worksheets, alternating with three units devoted entirely to rhythmic and melodic sight-reading exercises—allows a high degree of flexibility and has proved an invaluable feature of the book. This organization remains intact in this edition.

In other respects, many changes have been made to strengthen and improve the book. The discussion of certain topics has been revised and reordered for greater clarity and simplicity. New worksheets have been added and others have been revised. Unit 8 has been divided into two revised units. Unit 8 now covers melodic writing and transposition and Unit 9 focuses on harmonization and chord progressions. The text units present notation, meter, scales and modes, intervals, triads, seventh chords, the basic principles of melodic writing and transposition, and harmonization and accompaniment. As with a foreign language, music must be experienced, not simply read about; therefore, the verbal explanations are brief and the music examples are copious.

Units 1, 3, 4, 6, 8, and 9 end with numerous worksheets, keyed in the margin to the corresponding text sections for the students' convenience in review. These worksheets, including an overall review test, recapitulate the entire contents of each unit and offer more than enough practice to give students ease and confidence with each theoretical concept.

Units 2, 5, and 7 present a large number of sight-reading exercises, carefully graded from easy to challengingly difficult. Each unit contains one-, two-, and three-part rhythmic exercises, one- and two-part melodic exercises, valuable coordinated melodic-rhythmic exercises, and rhythmic and melodic dictation examples, all of which include and reinforce the material in the text units. The students learn to count both divi-sions and subdivisions of the beat, and they learn four ways of singing the melodic exercises—by pitch name, by scale-degree number, and by either movable or fixed solfeggio syllables. The sheer quantity of these exercises is one of their greatest virtues.

Many of the early examples in Unit 2 are readily adaptable to classroom dictation. For the rhythmic dictation, the instructor can first name the note value to be used as the unit of beat, establish the meter and tempo by clapping two or three preliminary bars, and then clap the exercise, with the students writing the note values they hear and adding bar lines. This process should be repeated no more than three times for each exercise. This approach can be similarly adapted to the melodic exercises. At first, the combination of rhythmic and melodic elements may pose too many problems. In such cases, the instructor may ignore meter signatures and note values, playing the melodies slowly, with an equal value for each note, and announcing both the first note and the clef. Later, when the students have gained ability and confidence in handling rhythm and melody separately, instructors can combine the two elements. The melodic examples in Unit 2 are also appropriate for the practice of transposition.

Periodically, measures are left blank. This offers students an opportunity to be more creative and, at the same time, provides a successful technique for learning to read music. After students have completed the work assigned in Unit 2, the instructor may place several of their examples on the board, clap or sing the examples, and then discuss reasons for one being more appropriate than another. The benefits from these exercises will far outweigh the extra time in class instruction they may entail.

The organization of the book allows instructors to introduce subjects in whatever order they wish. Each unit is planned for a flexible approach. For example, the book presents two ways of constructing scales, two ways of constructing intervals, and two ways of transposing a melody. Furthermore, the book includes more material than instructors can probably cover in most one-semester courses—such as the introduction to twelve-tone technique in Unit 3, the information about commercial chords in Unit 6, and some of the most difficult exercises in Unit 7. Besides its obvious usefulness in the two-semester sequence, this material is included to motivate and challenge students to continue their exploration of these subjects on their own.

I extend my sincere thanks to my many friends for their support; to the Los Angeles Valley College music faculty and staff; to Los Angeles Valley College professor Richard Kahn for his kind contribution; and a very special thanks for my colleague and friend, Los Angeles Valley College instructor Chauncey Maddren, for his invaluable contributions and time spent in preparation of this sixth edition.

I also want to thank those who reviewed the manuscript for their helpful comments. They are Kevin J. McCarthy of University of Colorado-Boulder, Lynn Shuntleff of Santa Clara University, Thomas Sovik of University of North Texas, Wesley Abbott of Los Angeles City College, Arthur Unsworth of Appalachian State University, and Mark Polanka of DePaul University.

Thanks also go to the Wadsworth editorial group: Clark Baxter, Sharon Adams Poore, Kasia Zagorski, and Jonathan Katz; to the production/manufacturing group: Dianne Toop and Robert King of Wadsworth and Bonnie Balke of A-R Editions, Inc.; to Mark Orr, Marketing Manager; and to Jennifer Ellis, TPM, for her work on the web site.

Most of all, I'd like to thank the students who have in the past helped and inspired me in the development of this textbook.

Unit 1

The Basics

1a THE STAFF—STAVE(S)

The **staff** is a series of five lines and four spaces on which notes are written. A four-line staff is still in use for the notation of Gregorian chant (the chant of the Roman Catholic Church), but all other conventional notation always uses the five-line staff. Lines and spaces of the staff, for identification, are numbered from bottom to top. The term **stave** is seldom used in the singular form; however, it is often used in the plural form (e.g., one *staff*, two *staves*).

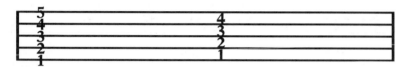

1b CLEFS

A **clef** is a sign written at the beginning of the staff to indicate the pitch name—A, B, C, D, E, F, or G—for a given line. There are three clef signs, representing the pitches G, F, and C, and the shapes of the signs are modifications of the shapes of these letters. The variety of clefs and clef positions results from the desire to avoid too many ledger lines (see 1c1). Whenever the range of a voice or instrument exceeded the five-line staff, composers or music copyists would change the position of the clef or introduce another clef. In the following list of clefs, the arrow indicates the position of middle C (the C nearest the middle of the piano keyboard) as it is notated in each clef.

(1) G CLEF (TREBLE CLEF)

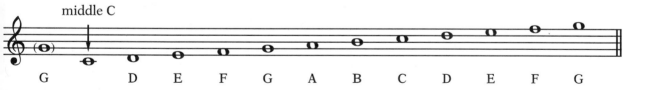

(2) F CLEF (BASS CLEF)

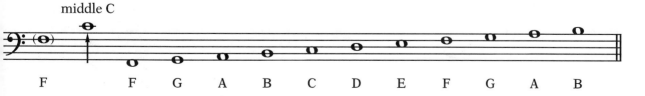

(3) C CLEF

Although in early music the G and F clefs were movable, they are now stationary. The C clef remains movable from one line to another, allowing the notes to remain within the staff. All five C clefs were commonly used until the middle of the eighteenth century, when composers gradually abandoned all but two of the positions: the alto and the tenor. The alto clef is still used to notate music for the viola, and the tenor clef is occasionally used for the cello, string bass, viol, bassoon, and trombone. The center of the curved line indicates the placement of middle C.

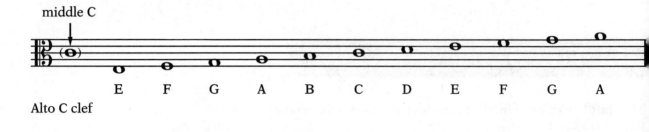

Alto C clef

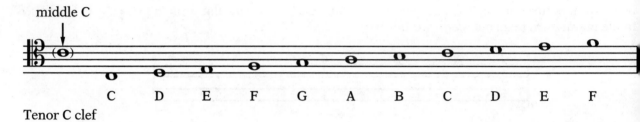

Tenor C clef

The following C clefs are seldom used.

Baritone C clef   Mezzo-soprano C clef   Soprano C clef

(4) DRAWING THE CLEFS

Treble Clef

Draw a vertical line.

Draw a curved line ending at the fourth line up.

Beginning with the fourth line, complete the clef by forming an incomplete circle in the bottom two spaces. The circle designates the note G.

2

Bass Clef

Beginning on the fourth line, draw a curved line to the right, ending on the second line directly under the beginning point.

Place two dots to the right of the clef above and below the fourth line. The dots designate the note F.

C Clef

The original C clefs were literally the letter C. We now form this clef by drawing a stylized letter C that delineates the line we wish to designate as C.

1c EXTENDING THE STAFF

(1) LEDGER LINES

For notes beyond the range of the five-line staff, small line segments called **ledger lines** are added above or below the staff, so that higher or lower notes may be written. Ledger lines are spaced with the same distance between them as that between the lines of the staff. They are just wide enough to extend slightly to the left and right of the note.

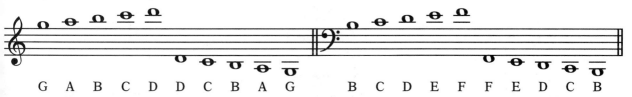

The note is placed on the last ledger line or in the space beyond the last ledger line. A ledger line is *never* used beyond the note.

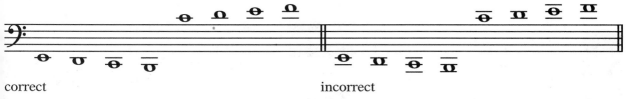

correct   incorrect

(2) OCTAVE SIGN (*8va*)

The range of the staff can be further extended with the **octave sign *8va***, indicating that the notes in the bracket are to be played an octave higher or lower. An octave is the pitch with the same name eight notes above or below the given pitch. The octave sign ***15ma*** indicates two octaves or fifteen pitches higher. The octave sign *8va* below a group of notes is not used in the treble and C clefs, and *15ma* below a group of notes is extremely rare.

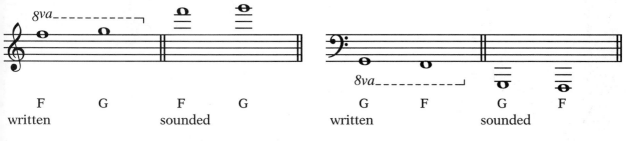

1d THE GREAT STAFF

The **great staff** (or grand staff) is a double staff with both a treble clef and a bass clef. All the most frequently used pitches can be written on this staff. Middle C is placed between the two staves. The great staff can be considered an eleven-line staff with middle C occupying the short eleventh line, or ledger line.

The piano keyboard is arranged in a pattern of seven white and five black keys and is repeated seven times on the modern 88-key piano. The black keys are in repeated patterns of two and then three. The note C is the first white key to the left of the two black keys. Western music divides the pitch into half steps (semitones): one key to the next *closest* key, white to black, black to white, and in the case of E-F and B-C, white to white. (See 1k.)

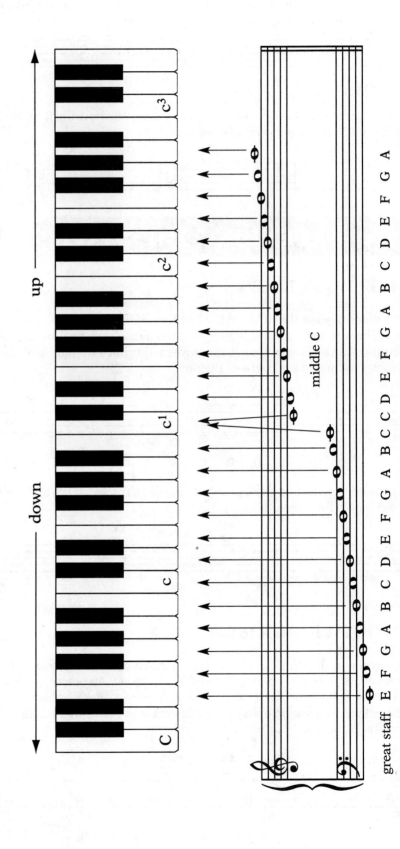

4

1e NOTES

(1) NOTE SYMBOLS

Notes are symbols indicating the relative duration and pitch when placed on a staff. Beginning with the whole note, each succeeding note is divided by two.

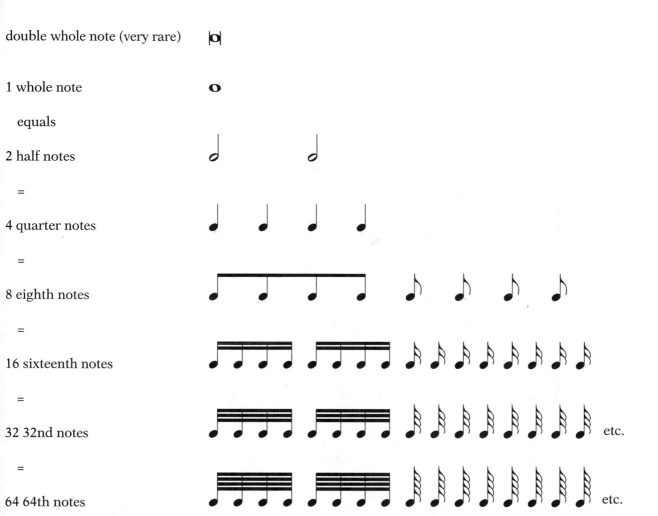

double whole note (very rare)

1 whole note

   equals

2 half notes

=

4 quarter notes

=

8 eighth notes

=

16 sixteenth notes

=

32 32nd notes   etc.

=

64 64th notes   etc.

(2) DOTTED NOTES

A dot after a note adds one half to the durational value of the note.

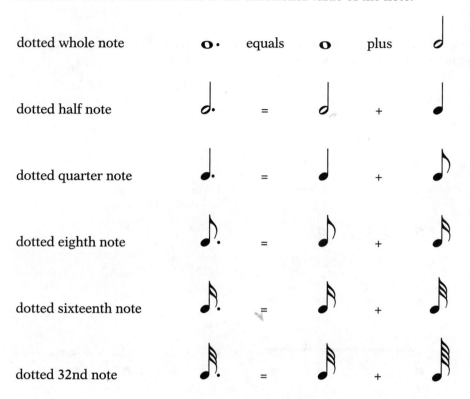

A double dot may be added to a note. It adds one half plus one quarter to the value of the note.

The dot is always added to the right side of the note. If the note is on a line, the dot is placed in the space above. If the note is in a space, the dot is placed in the same space.

(3) STEMS

As you just saw, all notes except whole notes have **stems.** Stems are drawn down if notes are above the middle line of the staff, and up if notes are below the middle line. Stems drawn up are placed on the right side of the note; stems drawn down are placed on the left side. The stem is usually an octave in length and, in notes using ledger lines, the stem extends to the middle staff line. For the middle-line note, stems may go up or down, but down is more usual.

(4) FLAGS

Flags (or hooks) denote values shorter than a quarter note; they always extend to the right of the stem. Eighth notes have one flag, sixteenth notes have two flags, 32nd notes have three, and 64th notes have four.

(5) BEAMS

In instrumental music, and increasingly in vocal music, it is customary to use **beams**—horizontal lines—in place of flags for groups of eighth, sixteenth, 32nd, and 64th notes. The number of beams corresponds to the number of flags: one beam for eighth notes, two for sixteenth notes, and so on. Beams can be used with notes of different values, as long as they have values shorter than a quarter note. The combined note value of the beamed notes will generally equal a single beat as indicated by the meter signature (e.g., in 𝄴 the combined beamed notes will equal one quarter note).

In beaming several notes together, place the beam above if the majority of stems would normally go up. If the majority of stems would normally go down, the beams are placed below. If there is no majority, use the direction of the note farthest from the middle line of the staff. Beams should more or less reflect, in a straight line, the overall contour of the note group.

(6) TIES AND SLURS

The **tie** is a curved line connecting two or more notes of the *same pitch*. The tie allows a note to be sustained across a bar line and is frequently used to arrive at a note total that is not otherwise available—a quarter note tied to a dotted quarter note, for example, produces a five-eighth note. The tied notes are not articulated but are sustained as a single note reflecting the sum of the tied notes.

A tie is necessary if a note is held beyond a bar line or if the same note is connected across two or mor measures.

A curved line placed above or below a group of notes of different pitch is called a **slur.** It indicates tha the notes are to be performed *legato*, smoothly connected with no breaks between them.

1f RESTS

Rests indicate silence. Each note value has its corresponding rest sign. The whole rest and half rest ar placed in the third space on the staff: the whole rest in the top half of the space and the half rest in th bottom half of the space. Rests are never tied, since a succession of rests produces an uninterrupte silence without any additional sign. Dotted rests are usually avoided. A rest for the note and an addi tional rest for the dot are preferred.

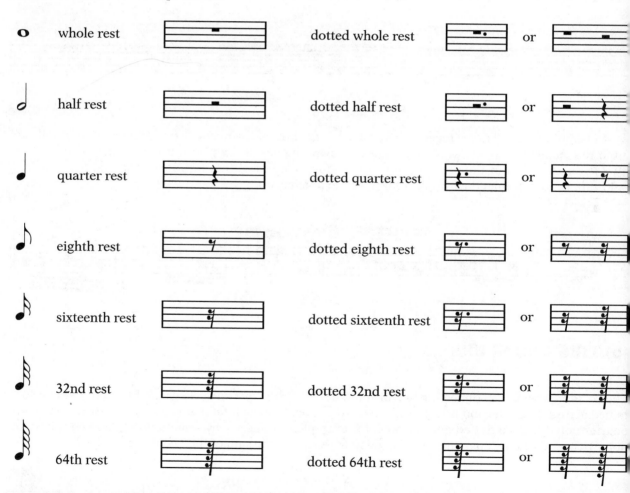

A whole rest serves as a full measure rest in any and all meters. Double-dotted rests are possible but rare. As with notes, the double dot adds one half plus one quarter value to the rest.

In ensemble music, parts may have several measures of rest at a time. A long rest sign, with a number above, indicates the number of measures of rest. The rest sign is drawn through the center line.

8-measure rest

1g METER SIGNATURES

The **meter signature** (or time signature) at the beginning of a piece indicates a recurring pattern of accented and unaccented *beats* (or *pulses*) that generally remains unaltered throughout a piece of music. The top number of the meter signature indicates the number of beats in the pattern, and the bottom number indicates the note (or rest) value of the beat. The recurring patterns are grouped into *bars*, or *measures*, and are separated from each other on the staff by *bar lines*.

(1) ACCENTED AND UNACCENTED BEATS

The first beat in each bar, often called the downbeat by musicians, receives the main accent or stress ('). Sometimes another beat or other beats in the bar receive a secondary stress (–). The remaining beats are unstressed (∪).

2 → two beats in the bar
4 → quarter note gets one beat

3 → three beats in the bar
8 → eighth note gets one beat

4 → four beats in the bar
4 → quarter note gets one beat

Note the secondary stress in this example.

Meter signatures generally fall into two categories. Basically, simple meters divide the beat into two compound meters divide the beat into three. Further subdivision for both meter types subdivide int multiples of two.

Following is a list of the most common simple and compound meters, with stressed and unstresse beats indicated.

(2) SIMPLE METERS

C Common Meter—symbol and name for $\frac{4}{4}$

¢ Cut Time (alla breve)—symbol and name for $\frac{2}{2}$

3) COMPOUND METERS

Compound meters, such as $\frac{6}{8}$, $\frac{9}{8}$, and $\frac{12}{8}$, differ from the preceding simple meters in that the beat divides into groups of *three*.

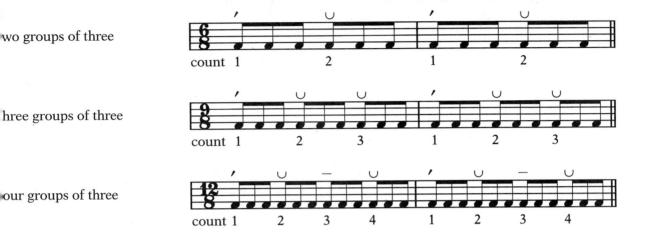

In compound meters played at a slow tempo, or speed, the eighth note receives one beat, the quarter note receives two beats, and the dotted quarter note receives three beats.

In a fast tempo, which is more usual for compound meters, the dotted quarter note receives one beat, the dotted half note receives two beats, and the tied dotted half and dotted quarter receive three beats.

But the most important thing to remember about compound meters is how they differ from simple meters. It is easy to distinguish the two types by remembering that simple meters divide the beat into groups of *two*, while compound meters divide the beat into groups of *three*.

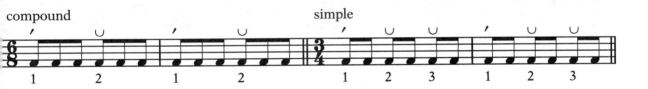

(4) UNEQUAL METRICAL DIVISIONS

In twentieth-century music, meter signatures with **unequal divisions** of the measure, such as $\frac{5}{4}$, $\frac{5}{8}$, $\frac{7}{4}$, and $\frac{7}{8}$, are widely used. $\frac{5}{8}$ and $\frac{7}{8}$ can be clearly defined by the use of beams.

The possibilities for other unequal divisions are limited only by the composer's imagination.

(5) TRIPLETS AND DUPLETS

A *triplet* is a "borrowed" grouping of three in an otherwise normal pattern of division by two. Triplets are indicated by a *3* placed above or below the beamed three-note group or with a bracket. Any note value may be used to form triplets, although the eighth-note triplet is the most often used. What all triplets have in common is that their total duration is equal to the duration of one note of the *next larger value.*

normal division   triplet division

The following example is written in ²₄ meter with triplets, and then in ⁶₈ meter. Both versions sound exactly the same; only the notation differs. By the use of the triplet, simple meters can be made to sound like compound meters.

simple

compound

A *duplet* is a "borrowed" grouping of two in an otherwise normal pattern of division by three (compound meters). Duplets are indicated by a bracket and a *2* over the notes. Any note value may be used to form duplets, although the eighth-note duplet is most often used.

normal division   duplet division

The following example is written first in $\frac{6}{8}$ meter with duplets and then in $\frac{2}{4}$ meter. Both versions sound exactly the same; only the notation differs. By use of the duplet, compound meters can be made to sound like simple meters.

compound

simple

1h DOUBLE BARS

A **double bar** is placed at the end of a work. It consists of a narrow bar line and a wider bar line.

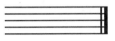

A double bar with two narrow bar lines designates the end of part of a work or section, but not the final close.

1i THE ANACRUSIS

A composition does not always begin on the first beat of the first measure. One or several notes can occur beforehand. These additional notes are called an **anacrusis** (or upbeat or pick-up note[s]). In vocal music, an anacrusis occurs when one or more unstressed syllables appear before the first stressed syllable.

The / cow jumped / over the / moon.

Formerly, the number of beats or the fraction of a beat used in the anacrusis was subtracted from the last measure of the work; in some cases, modern practice utilizes a complete final measure.

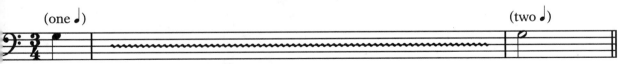

Accidentals are sharps, flats, or naturals introduced within the body of a work—in contrast to t[...] sharps or flats found in the key signature. An accidental is always placed in front of the note it affec[...] (i.e., on the same line or space as the note to which it refers).

A **sharp** (♯) raises the pitch of a tone by a half step. A **flat** (♭) lowers the pitch of a tone by a half step. Half steps may be either chromatic or diatonic (see 1k).

A **natural** (♮) is used to cancel a sharp or flat within a measure.

Except for the sharps and flats in the key signature (3d), the bar line cancels all accidentals in a previous measure.

Except for sharps and flats in the key signature (3d), an accidental affects a note only in the measure in which it appears, and only on that one line or space. For example, the second note in this measure is F♮, but the third note is F♯.

A **double flat** (♭♭) lowers the pitch of a tone by two half steps.
A **double sharp** (𝄪) raises the pitch of a tone by two half steps.

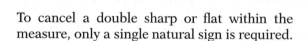

To cancel a double sharp or flat within the measure, only a single natural sign is required.

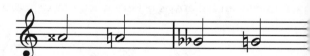

To cancel part of a double sharp or flat, a natural sign and the sharp or flat sign may be used but is not necessary. A single sharp or flat is sufficient.

1k HALF STEPS AND WHOLE STEPS— CHROMATIC OR DIATONIC

In most Western music, the smallest interval, or distance, between two tones is a **half step** (semitone).

Two consecutive half steps combined make a **whole step.** Looking at the piano keyboard, you will notice a black key between C and D. The distance from C up to that black key is a half step. From the black key to D is a second half step. The two half steps combined result in a whole step. The nearest key, black or white, above or below any other key is a half step. Therefore, the next white key above B or E, or below C or F, is a half step.

Half steps may be either *chromatic* or *diatonic*. Chromatic half steps employ the same letter name (e.g., F to F♯ or B to B♭). Diatonic half steps employ adjacent letter names (e.g., F to G♭ or B to A♯).

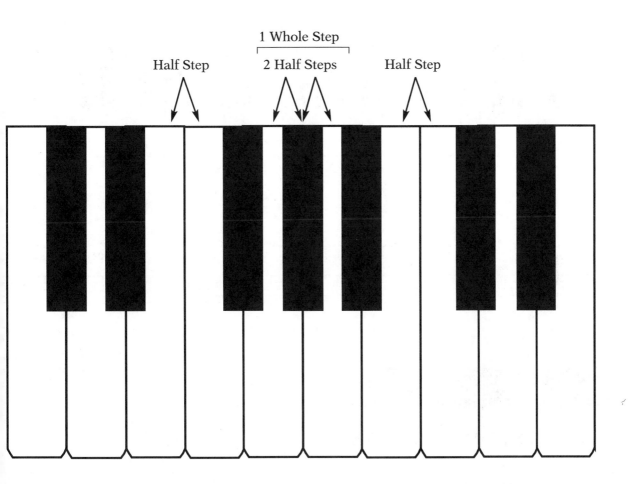

11 ENHARMONIC EQUIVALENTS

With the exception of G♯ and A♭, every tone can have three different names, as shown below. Tones that are named differently but that sound the same are called **enharmonic equivalents.**

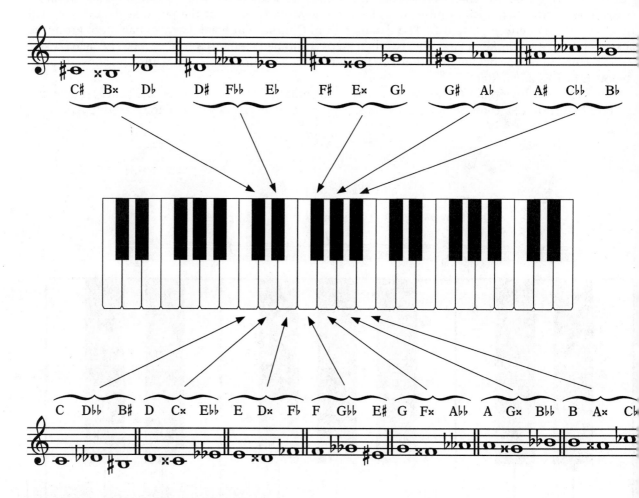

1m REPEAT SIGN

(1) D.C., D.S., CODA, AND *FINE*

Several kinds of **repeat signs** are used to direct the performer to skip back or forward through a work. These signs are used to avoid writing out long repeated passages.

D.C. (*da capo*)—repeat from the beginning
D.S. (*dal segno*)—repeat from the sign (𝄋)
fine—the end
D.C. al fine (*da capo al fine*)—repeat from the beginning to the end (the word *fine*)
D.S. al fine (*dal segno al fine*)—repeat from the sign (𝄋) to the end (the word *fine*)
coda—a section at the end of a work
D.C. al coda—repeat from the beginning to the coda sign (⊕) and then skip to the coda
D.S. al coda—repeat from the sign (𝄋) to the coda sign (⊕) and then skip to the coda

2) FIRST AND SECOND ENDINGS

Sometimes, when music repeats, first and second endings are used in order to save space. The first ending, which has a repeat sign, is played only the first time through. The second time through, the first ending is skipped over and the second ending is played.

is played

Another repeat sign, frequently seen in contemporary commercial music, is a sign indicating the repeating of one or two measures. In patterns that are repeated over and over, this method proves a time-saver for both the composer and the copyist. A one-measure repeat is represented by the sign placed inside one measure.

A two-measure repeat is represented by the sign bridging two measures, with a 2 placed above the staff.

17

1n KEYBOARD OCTAVE REGISTERS

The standard 88-key piano keyboard has eight A, B, and C keys and seven D, E, F, and G keys. To enable you to describe clearly which "A" you are discussing, each octave register (C–B) has been assigned a specific letter register. Beginning with one octave below middle C of the piano, lower-case letters are used for the ascending octaves and upper-case letters for the descending octaves.

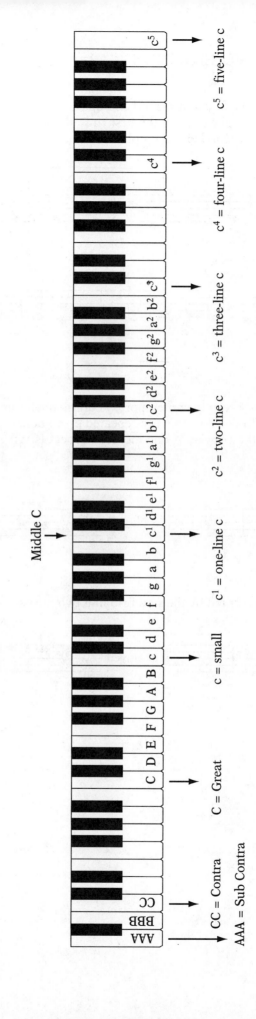

AAA = Sub Contra

CC = Contra

C = Great

c = small

c^1 = one-line c

c^2 = two-line c

c^3 = three-line c

c^4 = four-line c

c^5 = five-line c

Write the name of each of the following notes below the note or place the notes on the staff above the indicated names. In examples where two notes are available within the staff, write both notes.

Answer for line one.

19

NAME _____

Write the name of each of the following notes below the note or place the notes on the staff above the indicated names.

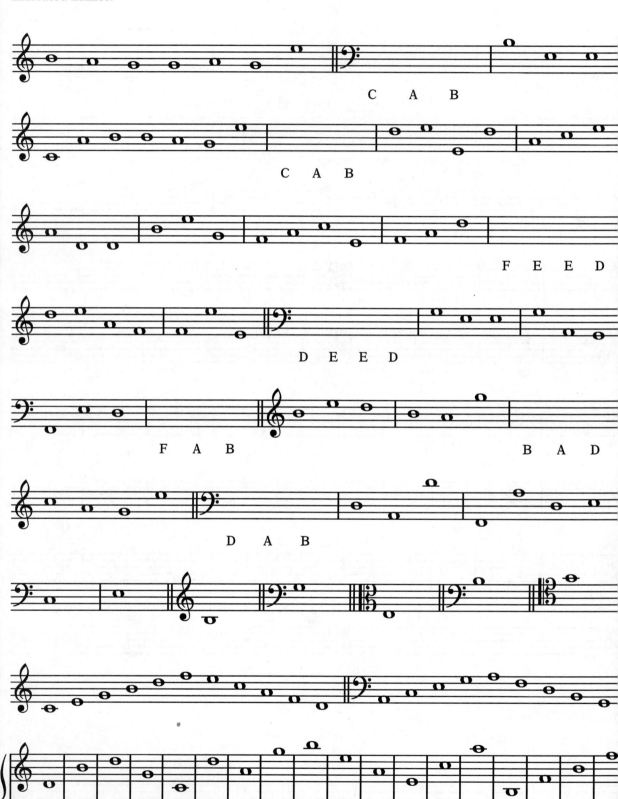

NAME _____

Write and name notes one octave *below* the given notes.

C   A   G   B
sample

Write and name notes one octave *above* the given notes.

D   B   F
sample

Add stems in the proper direction to the following note heads.

sample

Stem and beam the following notes in pairs of eighth notes.

sample

Stem and beam the following notes in groups of four sixteenth notes.

sample

NAME _____

1d
1l

Fill in the circles on the piano keyboard with the appropriate letter names and their enharmonic equiv
lents. (Refer to the keyboard at the end of the text.) Then write those notes on the Grand Staff below.
sure to note the placement of Middle C on the keyboard.

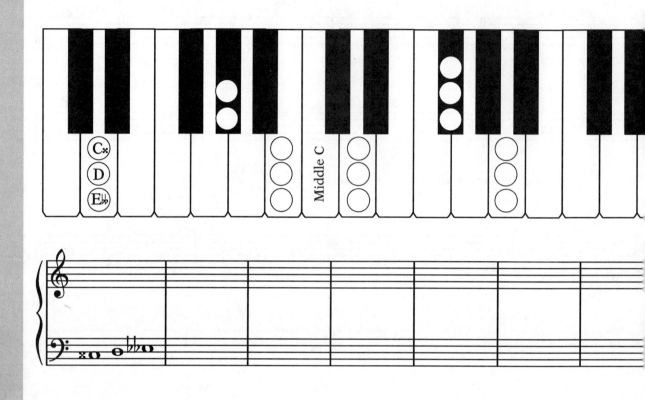

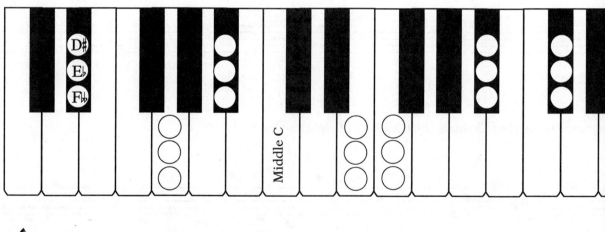

WORKSHEET 1-5   NAME _____

Divide the first note in each measure into the correct number of smaller notes indicated in parentheses.

1e
(1)
(2)

sample

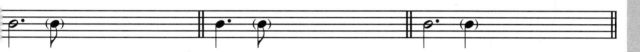

Write *one* note that is equal in length to the given notes. Use dots as necessary.

sample

23

1e
(6)

Give a simplified notation for the rhythms below, substituting *one note,* with a dot if necessary, for e
set of tied notes, as in the sample.

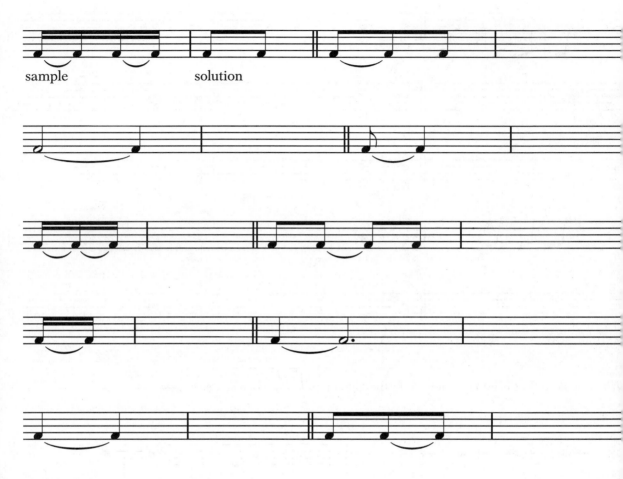

sample   solution

1f

Write the rest(s) that has (have) the same value as each of the following notes. For dotted notes, w
the equivalent rests *without using dots.*

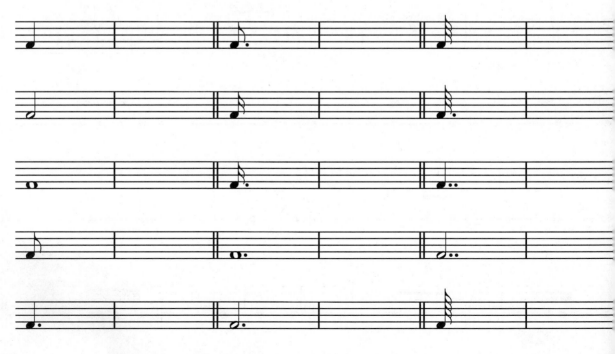

Write a note a diatonic whole step above and below the following notes.

sample

Write a note a diatonic half step above and below the following notes.

sample

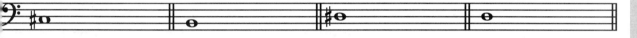

Write a note a chromatic half step above and below the following notes.

sample

Write the enharmonic equivalent for each of the following notes.

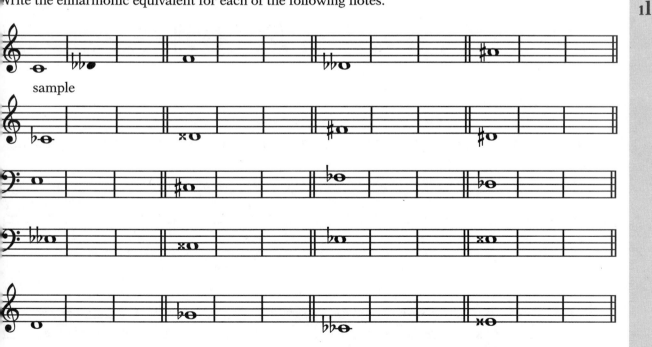

sample

1g   Place correct bar lines in each of the following rhythmic exercises. All examples begin on a downbeat.

Add a correct meter signature to each of the following measures.

Each of the following measures is rhythmically incomplete. Complete each measure by adding *one note* of the proper value, as in the sample. Do not place notes between two notes tied together.

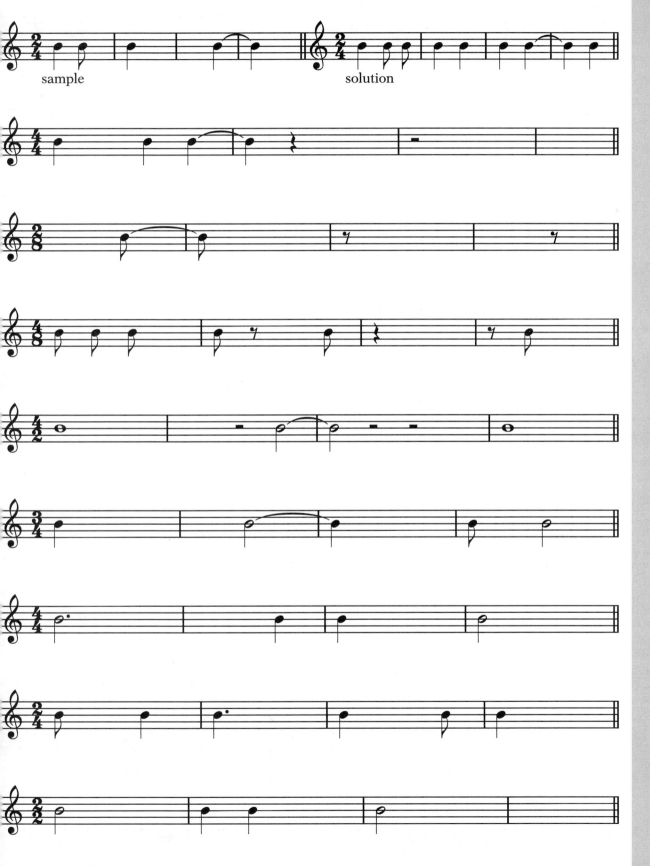

sample   solution

1. Write the name of each of the following notes below the note.

1b

1c

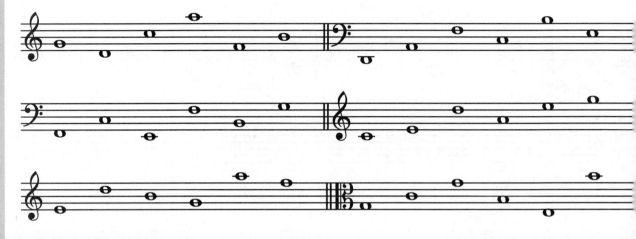

2. Divide the first note in each measure into the correct number of smaller notes indicated in parentheses.

1e
(1)
(2)

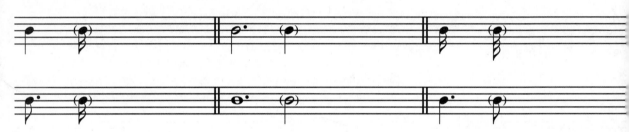

3. Write *one* note that is the durational equivalent of the note values shown. Use dots as necessary.

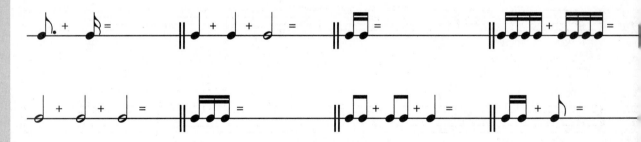

4. Write the rest(s) that has (have) the same value as each of the following notes. Do not use dotted rests.

1f

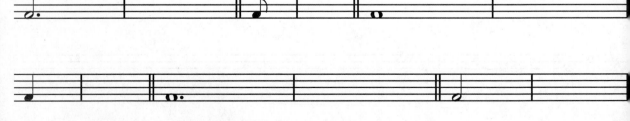

5. Write a note a diatonic whole step above and below the following notes.   **1k**

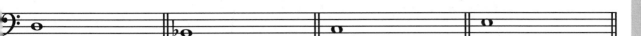

6. Write a note a diatonic half step above and below the following notes.

7. Write a note a chromatic half step above and below the following notes.

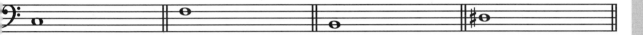

8. Write two enharmonic equivalents for each of the following notes.

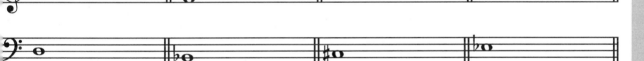   **1l**

9. Add a correct meter signature to each of the following measures. All examples begin on the down-beat.   **1g**

10. Place correct bar lines in the following rhythmic exercises.

Rhythmic and Melodic Exercises—Easy

2a RHYTHMIC EXERCISES: GROUP 1

The following suggestions will help you establish good practice habits in these rhythmic exercises.

- Before beginning, establish a moderate tempo, counting out loud or tapping your foot for at least two measures. On the metronome, a setting of 80 or 84 (that is, 80 or 84 beats per minute) will be comfortable. If you do not have a metronome, use a watch with a second hand and tap a bit faster than once per second. *Never practice too fast*; it is the downfall of all beginners.
- Clap the strong beats louder than the weaker beats. For notes with more than one beat, clap the first beat aloud and silently clap the remaining beats. In 4/4, for example, the whole note will be clapped aloud on one and silently clapped on two, three, and four.
- *Count out loud.* For notes that last more than one beat, count the first beat aloud and whisper the remaining beats. In the first few exercises, the beats that are to be silently clapped and whispered appear in parentheses. In later exercises, write the beat numbers below the notes only if absolutely necessary.

1) SIMPLE METERS WITH NO BEAT DIVISION, USING o, 𝅝, 𝅗𝅥, AND 𝅘𝅥

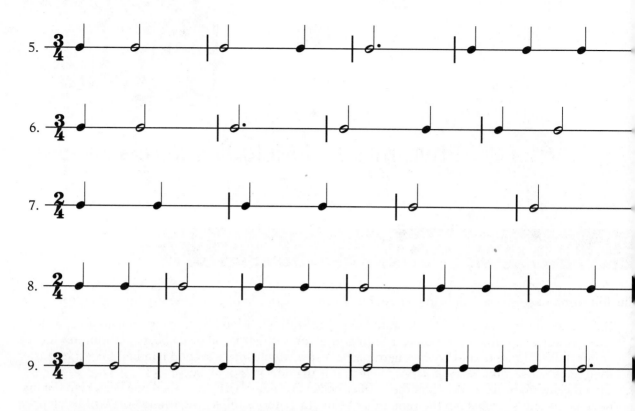

Periodically, measures will be left blank. Compose rhythms to complete the exercise.

Rhythm could be defined as a musically satisfying arrangement of note values within a basic pulse indicated by the meter signature.

Remember:
1. Limit note values to those found in this unit.
2. Be sure you have the combined note values indicated by the meter signature.
3. Look for rhythmic patterns that precede or follow the blank measures.
4. Compose rhythms that are consistent with the remaining measures of the exercise. In other words don't do something radically different from what is already there.

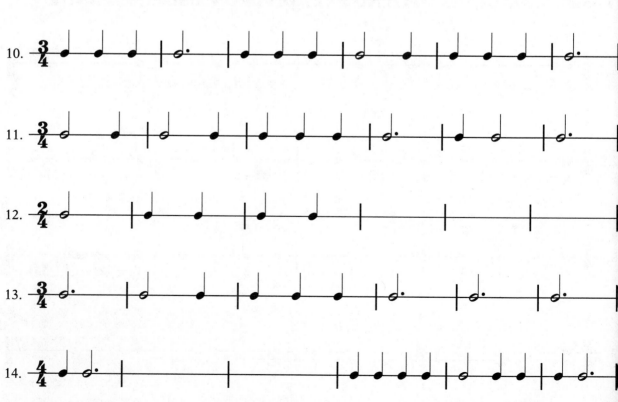

2) COORDINATED-SKILL EXERCISES

The following two-hand exercises will help you develop the skill of reading and performing two rhythmic patterns at the same time. On a table, desk, or your knee, tap the notes below the line with your left hand; then tap the notes above the line with your right hand. After tapping each line separately, tap them together. *Practice slowly.*

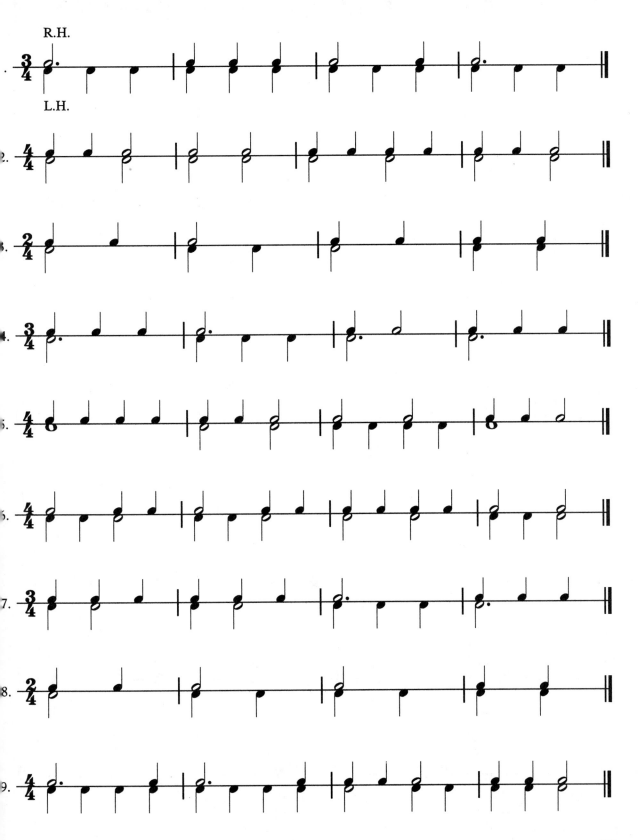

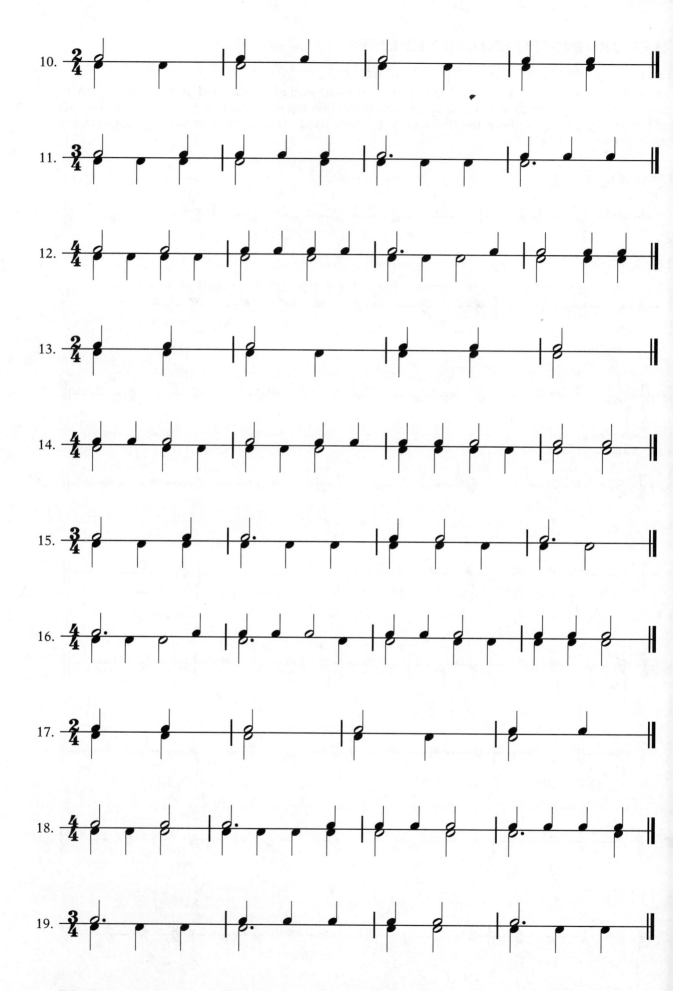

2b RHYTHMIC EXERCISES: GROUP 2

1) SIMPLE METERS WITH BEAT DIVISION;
EW MATERIAL—♪ AND ♫

counting simple meters, the division of the beat requires an additional word. Add the word *and* to the cond, weaker half of the beat, like this: "ONE-and *two*-and *three*-and," etc. When you tap your foot, the p down is the beat, the motion up is "and." Counting out loud will help you establish a stronger feeling rhythmic patterns. *Practice slowly.*

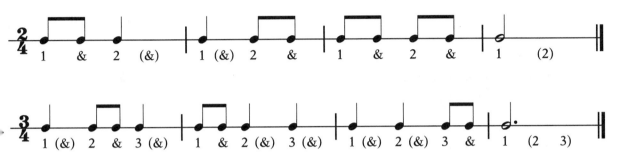

metimes the double bar with two dots is used in pairs to indicate a repeat. the measure(s) within the peat signs are played twice. The repeat signs always have two dots on the inside, facing the measure(s) be repeated. If the repeat is to the beginning of a work, a sign at the beginning is not required.

repeat signs

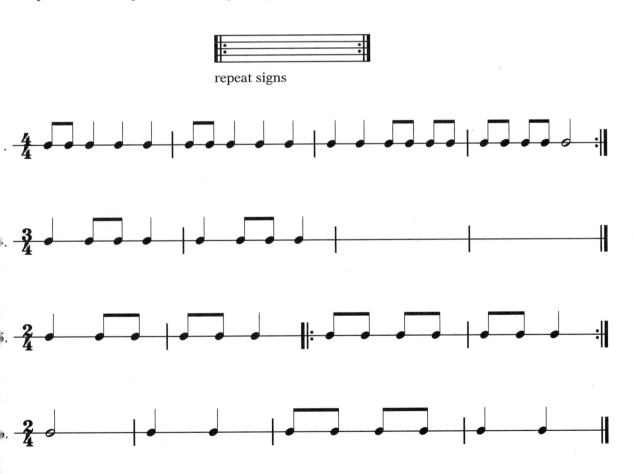

36

2) COORDINATED-SKILL EXERCISES

3) NEW MATERIAL—$\frac{2}{8}$, $\frac{3}{8}$, $\frac{4}{8}$, AND TIES

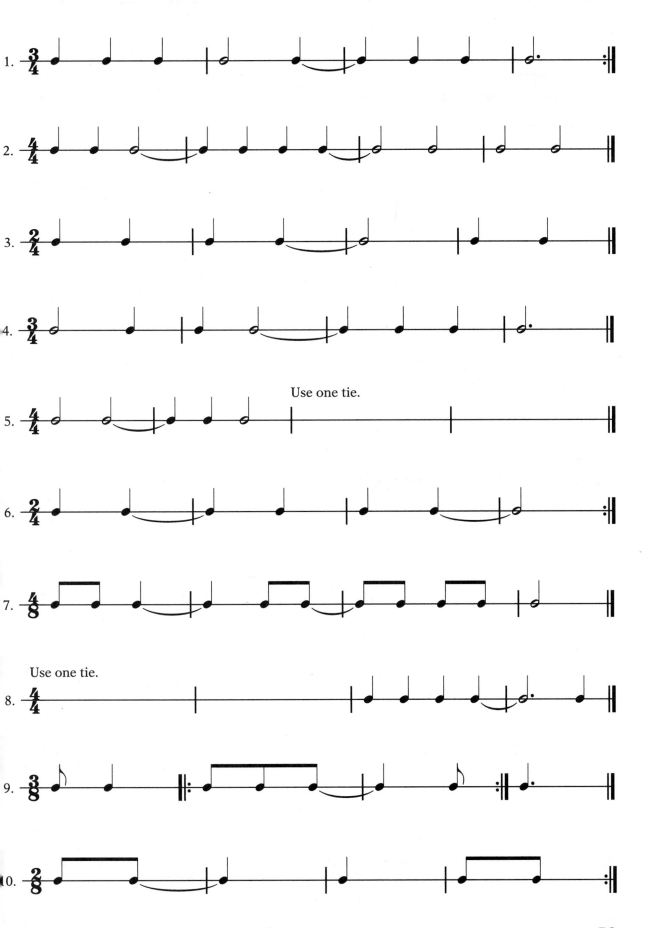

4) EIGHT-MEASURE EXERCISES

In writing eight-measure rhythmic exercises there are two possible approaches. Think of the first four measures as a question and the last four measures as an answer. The answer may be almost identical, as in example 2, or may be contrasting, as in example 5.

6. 4/4

7. 2/4

8. 4/8

9. 4/4

similar

or contrasting

(5) COORDINATED-SKILL EXERCISES

1. 2/4 R.H.

L.H.

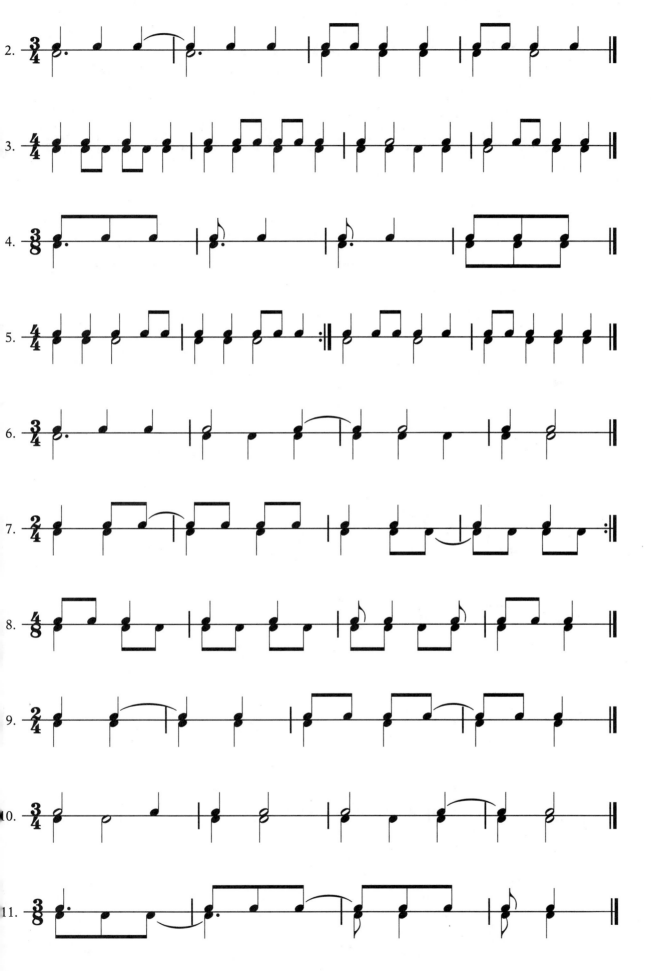

2c RHYTHMIC EXERCISES: GROUP 3

1) SIMPLE METERS WITH BEAT SUBDIVISION; NEW MATERIAL— ♪, ♫, AND ♩ ♪

In simple meters, the subdivision of the beat requires additional words. In the division of the beat, we added the word *and*. We now add the syllable *eh* between the beat and the word *and*, then the syllable *ah* after the *and*. In the subdivision of the quarter note, the word *and* remains on the second half of the beat. For an accurate performance of the dotted quarter and eighth (♩ ♪), count the division of the beat, tapping the note on the appropriate word ♩   ♪ in simple meters 2/4, 3/4, 4/4.

2) EIGHT-MEASURE EXERCISES

Use one tie.

(3) COORDINATED-SKILL EXERCISES

49

4) NEW MATERIAL—RESTS AND ANACRUSES

5) EIGHT-MEASURE EXERCISES

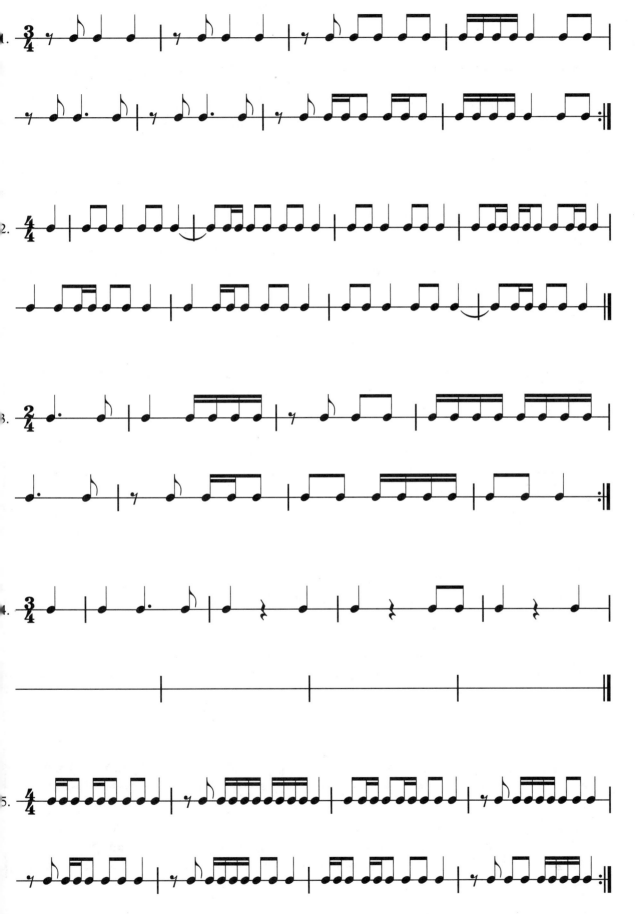

10. Use two rests.

5) COORDINATED-SKILL EXERCISES

(7) THREE-PART RHYTHMIC EXERCISES

These exercises are for group participation, with at least one person on each line. Divide the part among the performers, establish a beat, and begin. Perform each exercise a second and third time, with the performers tapping a different part each time.

You can use these exercises on your own to further develop your skill of reading multiple music lines. Practice lines 1 and 2, then lines 2 and 3, and then lines 1 and 3.

56

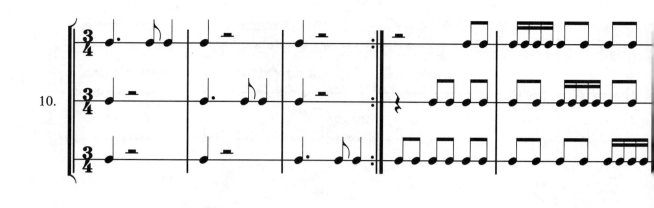

10.

11.

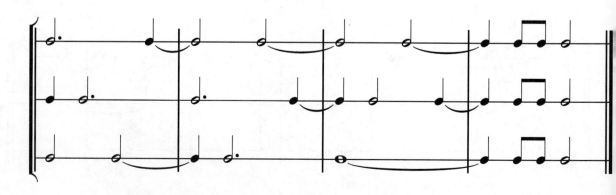

2d MELODIC EXERCISES: GROUP 1

he following suggestions will help you develop good practice habits in these singing exercises.

.   Each singing example should first be clapped as a rhythmic exercise.
.   It should then be sung, using the letter names of the notes (and singing it an octave higher or lower
    if it is uncomfortable for your range as written).
.   It should then be sung again, using the *number system,* in which the numbers 1-2-3-4-5-6-7 are
    assigned to the notes of the scale in any key (3a). For example: in the key of C, C is 1, D is 2, E is 3,
    etc; in the key of F, F is 1, G is 2, A is 3, etc.
.   Some suggestions about singing:
    Sit up straight or, better yet, stand while singing.
    Look straight forward with relaxed jaw and, if reading from music, hold music in front of you or
        place on a stand at eye level.
    Sing at a moderately loud volume so that you can clearly distinguish pitches. At any extreme range,
        high or low, sing softer.

1) SIMPLE METERS WITH NO BEAT DIVISION

2) TWO-PART MELODIC EXERCISES

(3) COORDINATED MELODIC-RHYTHMIC EXERCISES

Similar to the coordinated rhythmic exercises, these exercises combine two musical activities—this time, singing and clapping. Learn each line separately, then combine the two skills. If possible, sing the melodic line with pitch names or numbers, but if you find the combination of singing and clapping too difficult, sing the melodic line on a neutral syllable. *Practice slowly.*

2e MELODIC EXERCISES: GROUP 2

(1) SIMPLE METERS WITH BEAT DIVISION

Periodically, chord names and roman numerals will appear above and below a given melody. These allow a musician to add the correct chord (Units 6 and 9) accompaniment to a given melody. The letters placed above the music, a common practice in commercial music, indicate the chord to be used for that measure or beat. Uppercase letters are major triads (6a1). The roman numerals placed below the music, more common in the academic study of music, indicate a chord based on the diatonic scale. The following melody is in F Major. The F Major scale is numbered one through seven, one being F, two, G, three A, and so forth. In this example, I is an F chord, IV is a B♭ chord, and V is a C chord.

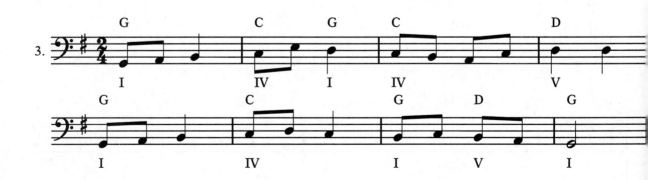

(2) TWO-PART MELODIC EXERCISE

1.

(3) COORDINATED MELODIC-RHYTHMIC EXERCISES

(4) EIGHT-MEASURE EXERCISES

Periodically, measures will be left blank. Compose melodies to complete the exercises.

Rhythm is equal in importance to the notes chosen for the melodic line. Before you begin, review the few simple rules for rhythms outlined on page 32.

All the following principles and rules of melodic writing are very general and many exceptions may be found with a continued study of music. For the beginner, the understanding of these basic principles and rules will be an introduction to the interesting mysteries of composing. More information on this subject, including harmonization, can be found in Units 8 and 9.

Basic Principles

Most music is written in an orderly fashion and will have certain patterns of construction. These patterns are called musical *form*. The smallest form is called a *phrase*.

Keeping in mind that there are many exceptions to these principles, phrases are usually four measures long. Two phrases combine to form a *period*.

The first phrase of a period is called the *antecedent* phrase, the second the *consequent* phrase.

Similar to the rules outlined for rhythms on page 32, the two phrases may take two basic forms—a *parallel* period, where the first and second phrases are nearly identical, and a *contrasting* period, where the first and second phrases are dissimilar. Example 2 is parallel in construction and example 6 is contrasting in construction.

Melodic lines may move by scale step (conjunct motion) or outline triads (6a) and wide interval leaps (disjunct motion).

Melodic lines have an overall "architecture." Two phrases may remain rather static, the first phrase ascend and the second descend, the first descend and the second ascend, or any combination of the above.

Basic Rules

1. The first phrase will usually end on a note other than the tonic (3a), the second almost always on the tonic.
2. Limit the number of rhythmic patterns.
3. Make the melody "singable." This is rather an abstract idea, but a good rule to follow. Sing your melody and if it feels comfortable it is likely to be correct.
4. Constrain the *tessitura,* that is, the overall range of notes from the lowest to the highest, to no more than an octave and a third.

(5) TWO-PART MELODIC EXERCISE

6) COORDINATED MELODIC-RHYTHMIC EXERCISES

73

2f MELODIC EXERCISES: GROUP 3

(1) SIMPLE METERS WITH BEAT DIVISION AND SUBDIVISION

Round Form

A round requires the performers to be divided into three or four equal groups. Each group will perform the complete work. The first group begins at the opening phrase (1), the second, starting at the beginning, enters when the first group reaches the second phrase (2), and so on. Rounds may be repeated as many times as you wish.

(2) TWO-PART MELODIC EXERCISE

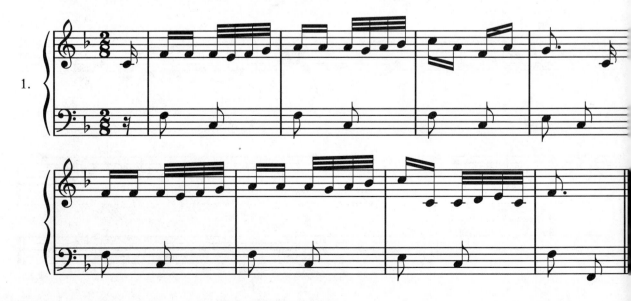

(3) COORDINATED MELODIC-RHYTHMIC EXERCISES

Unit 3

Scales, Keys, and Modes

3a SCALES

A **scale** (from Italian *scala*, ladder) is an ordered series of pitches, going either up or down. There are many forms of scales, but the two most commonly used in Western music since the seventeenth century are the forms called *major* and *minor*. The major scale is represented by the white keys of the piano that span the octave C to C. The ascending major-scale arrangement of whole steps and half steps is as follows: a whole step between the first and second and the second and third pitches, a half step between the third and fourth, a whole step between the fourth and fifth, the fifth and sixth, and the sixth and seventh pitches, then a half step between the seventh and eighth pitches. The following major scale is represented C to C.

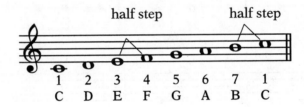

Each scale step has a name that indicates its relationship to the *tonic,* the name of the beginning note of the scale and main tone of the key.

> *tonic*—beginning pitch
> *supertonic*—the pitch *above* the tonic
> *mediant*—the pitch halfway between the tonic and the dominant
> *subdominant*—the dominant five pitches *below* the tonic or the pitch *below* the dominant
> *dominant*—the dominant five pitches *above* the tonic
> *submediant*—the pitch halfway between the tonic and the subdominant
> *leading tone*—half step *below* the tonic

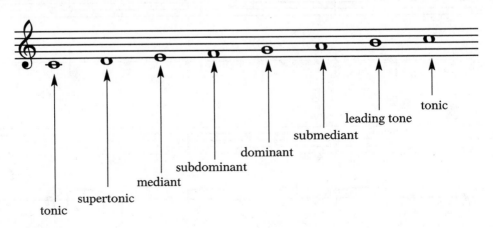

3b CIRCLE OF FIFTHS—MAJOR KEYS

A scale that follows the half-step and whole-step pattern described is called a major *diatonic* scale. With this half-step and whole-step pattern kept consistent, the major scale can be transposed (moved) to all the remaining eleven half steps within the octave. For each transposition, sharps or flats must be added to maintain the correct diatonic pattern.

The major scales and their appropriate sharps or flats can be arranged in a sequence called the **circle of fifths,** shown in the diagram below. With C at the top, the fifths lead clockwise to G, then to D, and so on around the circle. The key signature indicates whether the name of the new key will be sharped or flatted, e.g., the descending fifth below F is B. But the key signature, two flats, dictates that B will be flatted. Therefore the name of the new key is B♭. Note that the scales requiring sharps are clockwise *ascending* fifths, and that the scales requiring flats are counterclockwise *descending* fifths. Note also that at the bottom of the circle, the scales with sharps and flats must cross. These three sets of scales, each with two key signatures, are called *enharmonic* major scales. (See 1l.)

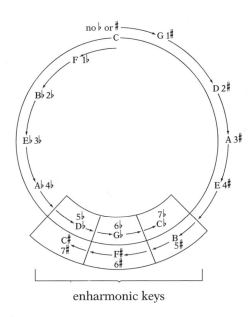

enharmonic keys

3c OVERTONES

The use of the fifth in the circle of fifths is not an arbitrary choice. Every pitch is a composite of sounds, consisting of the main sound (the *fundamental*) plus many more. Most of these additional sounds, called **overtones, harmonics,** or **partials,** are not distinctly heard; however, the first overtone, which is an octave above the fundamental, and the second overtone, which is a fifth plus an octave over the fundamental, are clearly audible. This fifth is a very dominant sound for every pitch of the scale.

To hear these two overtones, *silently* depress the white keys of the piano from C to C with your right hand. With your left hand, strike the C one octave lower a hard, short blow. You will hear the tones C and G distinctly. Then silently depress the white keys from G to G, strike the G one octave lower, and you will hear G and D. You can continue this procedure throughout the circle of fifths.

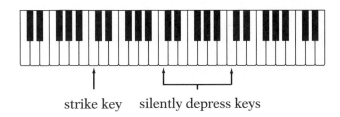

strike key   silently depress keys

3d KEY SIGNATURES

In music based on a major or minor scale, the piece often centers on a specific tone, the first note of the scale. This tone is called the *tonic* (or keynote or key center). Playing a G major scale or a piece using this scale means playing in the *key* of G major. The sharps or flats used in a particular key are grouped together at the beginning of the staff in an arrangement called the *key signature*. Any sharp or flat shown in the key signature means that the corresponding note is played sharped or flatted throughout a composition—although the sharp or flat may be canceled with a natural sign (♮) for a single measure (see 1j).

The sequence of sharps or flats in a *key signature* follows a specific order. The first sharp in all sharp key signatures, major or minor, is *always* F, the second sharp is *always* C, the third G, and so on. The first flat in all flat key signatures is *always* B, the second flat is *always* E, the third A, and so on. Therefore, the circle of fifths, shown above, indicates that the key of G has 1 ♯ and that sharp must be F. The key of F is shown to have 1 ♭ and that flat must be B.

Below you will find not only the correct key signature notation but the specific order that the sharps and flats must follow.

Please note that the sharp and flat key signatures also follow the circle of fifths. The sharps begin at F (11 o'clock) and move clockwise to B (5 o'clock). The flats simply reverse the order and begin with B (5 o'clock) and move counterclockwise to F (11 o'clock).

In notating key signatures, the sharps or flats are placed on the staff in a certain pattern that is never altered: In the treble clef, the first sharp, F, is always placed on the top line; in the bass clef, on the fourth line up. In the treble clef, the first flat, B, is always placed on the middle line; in the bass clef, on the second line up. The diagram below shows the placement of the remaining sharps and flats in the pattern that must always be followed. In notation, allow sufficient space so that none of the sharps or flats is directly above or below another.

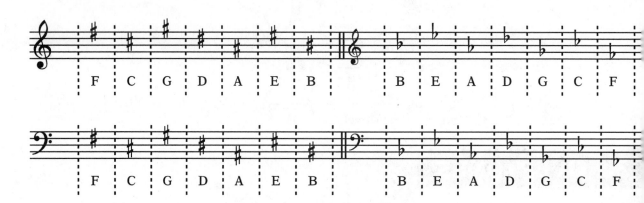

| F | C | G | D | A | E | B | | B | E | A | D | G | C | F |

| F | C | G | D | A | E | B | | B | E | A | D | G | C | F |

3e TETRACHORDS

Another way to construct scales is by the use of the tetrachord, a concept that dates back to ancient Greek music. The **tetrachord** is a four-note pattern of whole steps and half steps that, when combined with another tetrachord, forms a one-octave scale. The tetrachord for the major scale is a pattern of two whole steps followed by a half step. Starting with C, an ascending series of this pattern, with each tetrachord separated by a whole step, will result in the twelve major scales, the last leading back to C. Any two neighboring tetrachords in this pattern will spell a major scale, as in the diagram below. The minor scales and the modal scales (see 3o) can also be learned by memorizing their individual tetrachord patterns. Except for the Lydian mode, each tetrachord pattern will be separated by a whole step.

Major-Scale Tetrachord Series

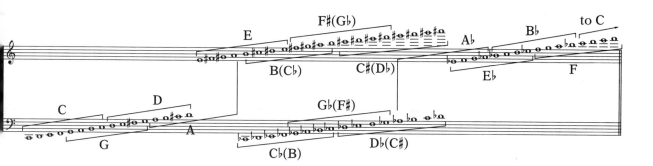

Refer to 3o for more information on the modes.

Major scale   1 2 3 ^4 / 5 6 7 ^8

Natural (unaltered) minor scale   1 2 ^3 4 / 5 ^6 7 8

Dorian mode   1 2 ^3 4 / 5 6 ^7 8

Phrygian mode   1 ^2 3 4 / 5 ^6 7 8

Lydian mode   1 2 3 4 /^5 6 7 ^8

Mixolydian mode   1 2 3 ^4 / 5 6 ^7 8

3f MAJOR SCALES WITH SHARPS

Following the circle clockwise from 11 o'clock (F) to 5 o'clock (B) will also give you the order of sharp found in sharp key signatures.

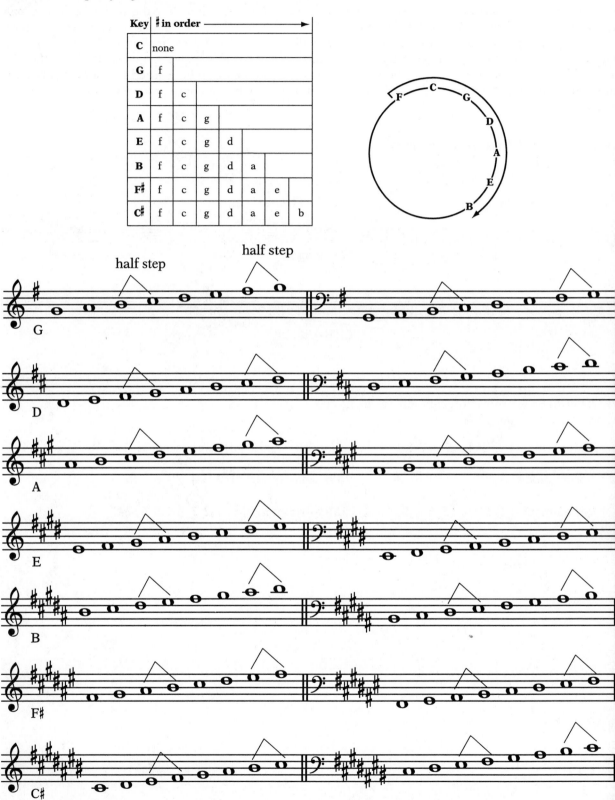

Key	# in order ———————————▶						
C	none						
G	f						
D	f	c					
A	f	c	g				
E	f	c	g	d			
B	f	c	g	d	a		
F♯	f	c	g	d	a	e	
C♯	f	c	g	d	a	e	b

Another way to identify the key of the scale is to remember that in key signatures with sharps, the note one diatonic half step above the last sharp in the key signature gives the name of the key.

3g MAJOR SCALES WITH FLATS

Following the circle counterclockwise from 5 o'clock (B) to 11 o'clock (F) will also give you the order of flats found in flat key signatures.

Key	b in order ⟶					
C	none					
F	b					
Bb	b	e				
Eb	b	e	a			
Ab	b	e	a	d		
Db	b	e	a	d	g	
Gb	b	e	a	d	g	c
Cb	b	e	a	d	g	c	f

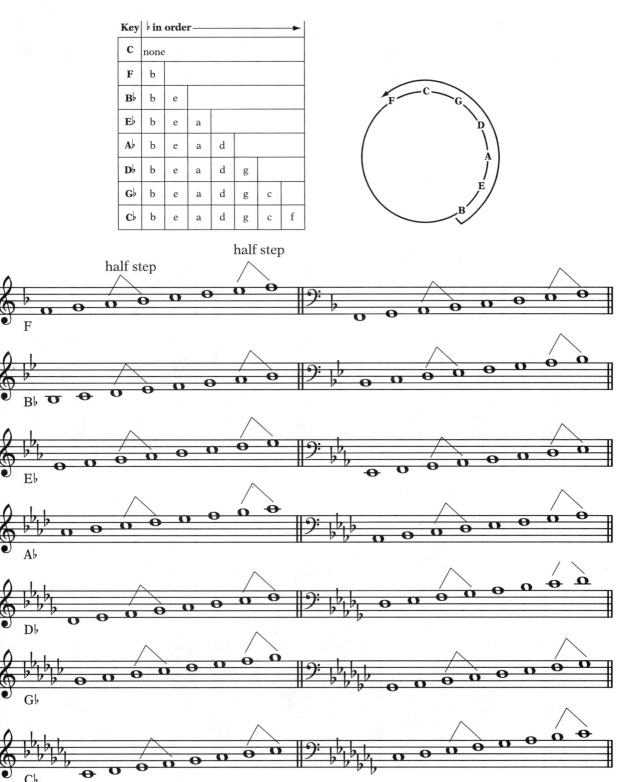

Another way to identify the key of the scale is to remember that in key signatures with flats, the name of the next-to-last flat gives the name of the key, except in the case of F, which has only one flat.

Below are shown three major scales, **C**, **A** and **E♭**, and how these scales appear on the piano keyboard.

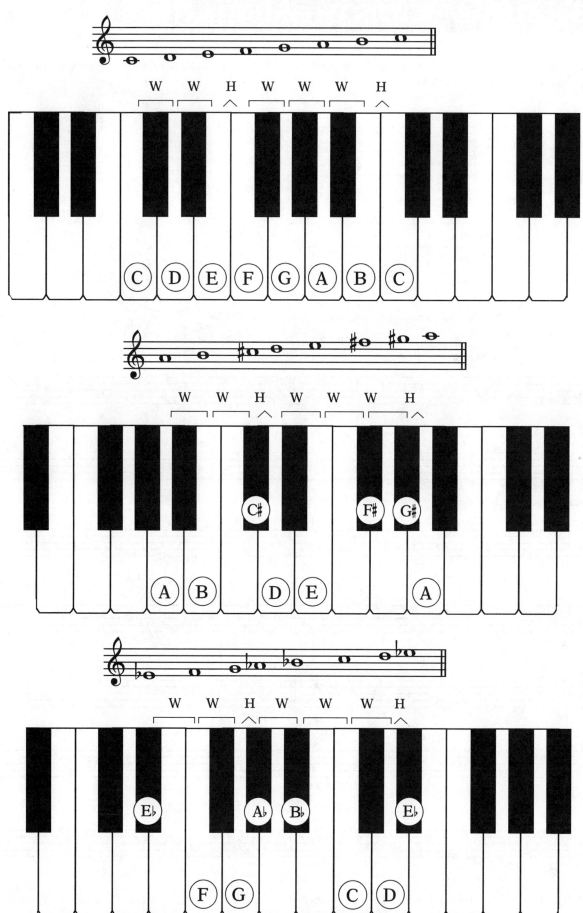

3h CIRCLE OF FIFTHS—MINOR KEYS

he rules that apply to the major circle also apply to the circle in minor, as shown in the diagram below.[*]
'he *natural* minor scale is represented by the white keys of the piano that span the octave A to A. Half
teps appear between the second and third pitches, and between the fifth and sixth. With this whole-step
nd half-step pattern kept consistent by adding sharps or flats, the minor scale can be transposed to all
ie remaining eleven half steps within the octave. The scales requiring sharps are clockwise *ascending*
fths, and the scales requiring flats are counterclockwise *descending* fifths.

The natural minor scale can be altered by adding accidentals, to produce two other forms—the *har-
zonic* and the *melodic* minor (see 3k).

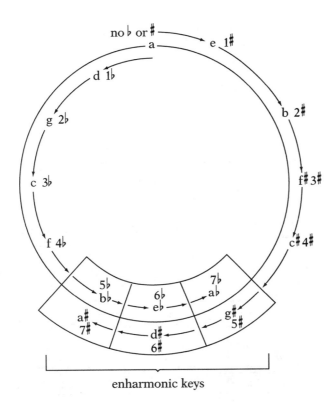

enharmonic keys

The use of lower-case letters in this diagram to refer to minor keys is a well-known convention, and one this book will use from now on. Thus, cap-
tal G in diagrams means G major and lower-case g means g minor.

3i MINOR SCALES WITH SHARPS

Following the circle clockwise from 8 o'clock (F) to 2 o'clock (B) will also give you the order of sharps found in sharp key signatures.

Key	# in order→					
a	none					
e	f					
b	f	c				
f#	f	c	g			
c#	f	c	g	d		
g#	f	c	g	d	a	
d#	f	c	g	d	a	e
a#	f	c	g	d	a	e	b

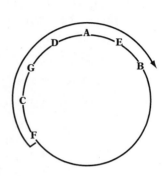

3j MINOR SCALES WITH FLATS

Following the circle counterclockwise from 2 o'clock (B) to 8 o'clock (f) will also give you the order of flats found in flat key signatures.

Key	♭ in order ——————→						
a	none						
d	b						
g	b	e					
c	b	e	a				
f	b	e	a	d			
b♭	b	e	a	d	g		
e♭	b	e	a	d	g	c	
a♭	b	e	a	d	g	c	f

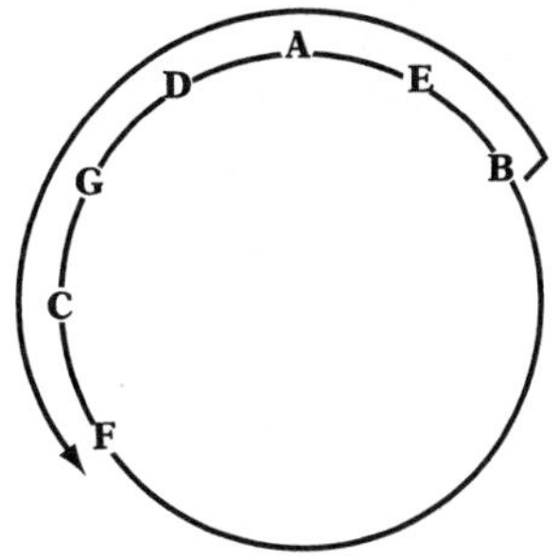

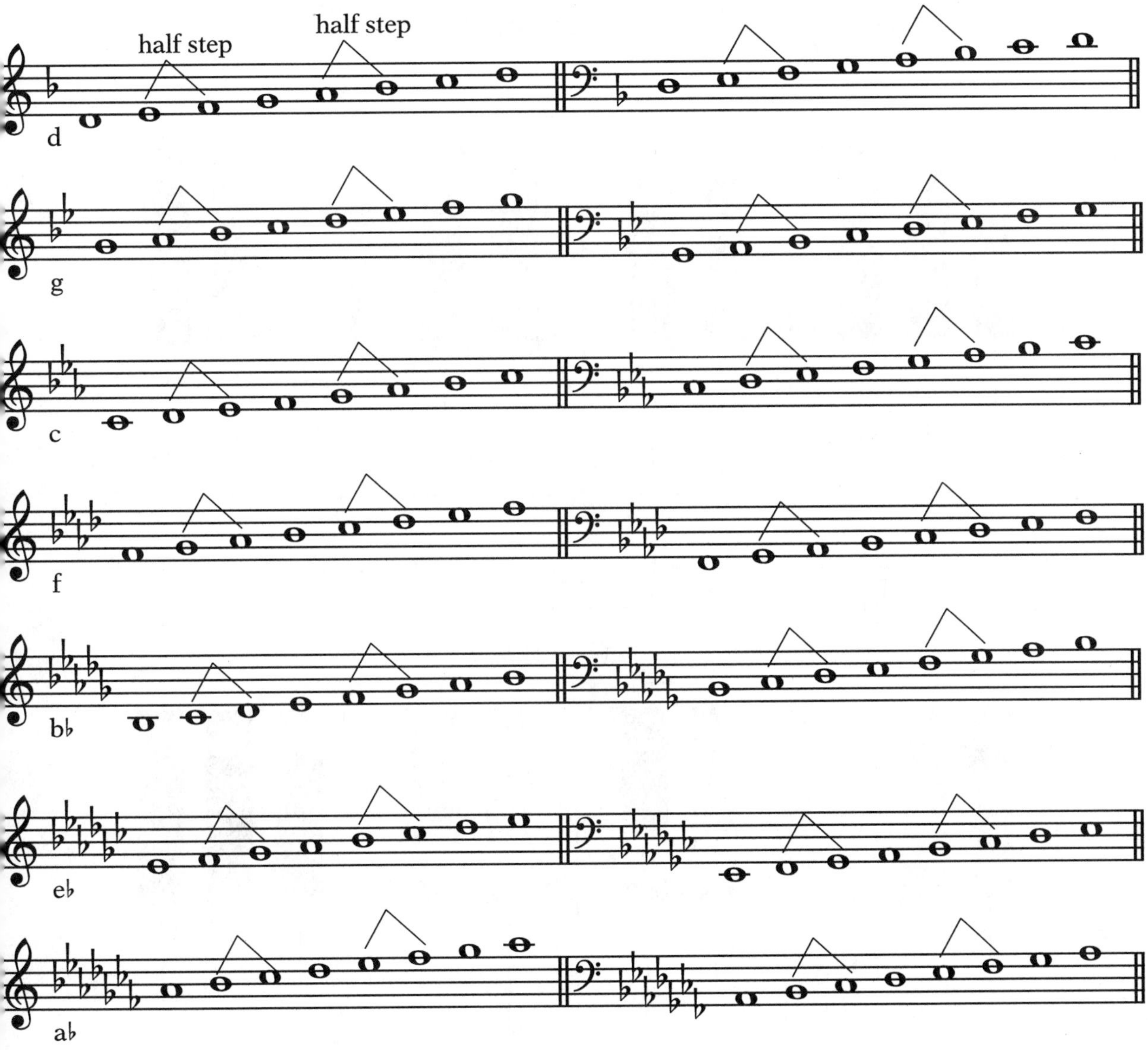

half step   half step

d

g

c

f

b♭

e♭

a♭

Below are shown three minor scales, **a, b,** and **f,** and how these scales appear on the piano keyboard.

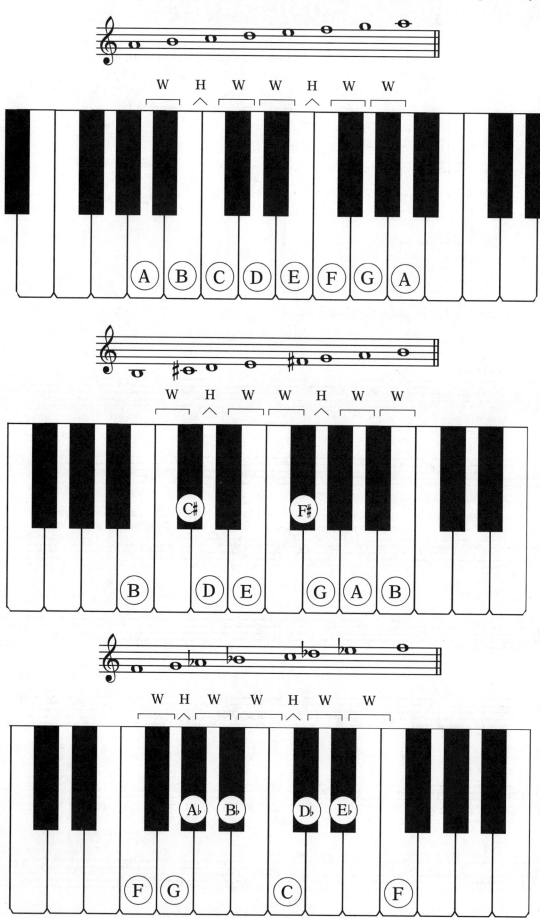

3k NATURAL, HARMONIC, AND MELODIC MINOR

The minor scale has three forms—the natural (unaltered) form, the harmonic form, and the melodic form. Each has its own unique characteristics. You should play and sing each form until you can recognize its distinct quality.

The **natural minor scale** is sometimes called the Aeolian, in reference to its origin as one of the church modes (see 3o).

natural minor

The **harmonic minor** scale raises the seventh pitch of the natural minor scale by one half step. This results in a skip of a step and a half between the sixth and seventh scale steps.

one and one-half steps

harmonic minor

The **ascending melodic minor** scale raises by one half step the sixth and seventh pitches of the natural minor scale. Descending, the sixth and seventh pitches are returned to their original pitches. The **descending melodic minor** scale, therefore, returns to the natural minor form.

ascending melodic minor   descending melodic minor (natural)

3l RELATIVE MAJOR AND MINOR

Major and minor keys with different names but with the same key signatures are called **relative.** To find the relative *minor* key of a major key, count down three degrees of the scale from the first note (the tonic) of the major scale, or count up six degrees of the scale from the tonic. To find the relative *major* key of a minor key, reverse the process: count down six degrees of the scale from the tonic, or count up three. In the following example, the key signature with one sharp applies to the keys of both G major and e minor.

Relative Major and Minor Key Signatures

count up 6

count down 3

92

3m PARALLEL MAJOR AND MINOR

Major and minor keys with different key signatures but with the same letter name and the same tonic are called **parallel.** The key signature of any parallel minor key is the same as that of its *relative* major. Find it by counting up three diatonic half steps, a minor third (or by counting down nine diatonic half steps). Counting up three, or down six, from G gives B♭, the relative major of g minor. Therefore two flats, the key signature of B♭, is also the key signature of g minor.

Another way to establish the parallel key signature is to move counterclockwise three places around the Circle of Fifths (3b); e.g., starting on G you move three spaces counterclockwise G–C–F–B♭ to get the key signature of the parallel minor.

Parallel Major and Minor Key Signatures

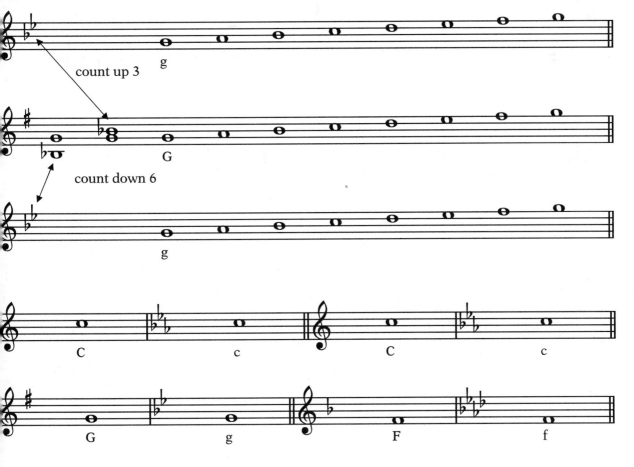

D   d   B♭   b♭

A   a   E♭   e♭

E   e   A♭   a♭

B   b   D♭   c♯

(spelled in its
enharmonic form—c♯)

F♯   f♯   G♭   f♯

(spelled in its
enharmonic form—f♯)

C♯   c♯   C♭   b

(spelled in its
enharmonic form—b)

3n THE CHROMATIC SCALE

hen any nondiatonic tones are introduced into a scale, they are called *chromatic* tones. The introduc-
on of every chromatic tone results in the **chromatic scale,** all the twelve tones within an octave. In
neral, sharps are used to notate the ascending scale; flats notate the descending scale. However,
arps or flats found in the key signature should be accounted for. Below is the *c* ascending and
scending chromatic scale, also the *F* ascending chromatic scale and the *G* descending chromatic
ale.

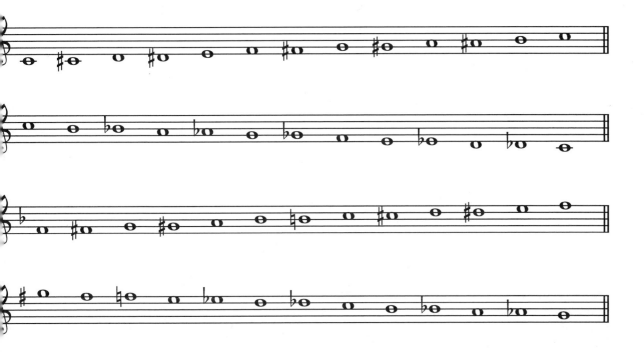

le white-key half-step pairs (E–F and B–C) are always notated as natural notes.

30 THE CHURCH MODES

The **church modes** were the tonal basis of early music until roughly the end of the sixteenth centur the end of the Renaissance. The modes are octave segments of the C major scale, each placing the ton on a different pitch in the scale (or white key on the piano). They appear on the staff as shown belo The major and minor scales replaced the modes and remained prominent until the late nineteenth ce tury, when composers rediscovered the early church modes and also became interested in other sca forms. The Dorian, Phrygian, Lydian, and Mixolydian modes remain in use today, the Dorian ar Mixolydian being especially popular with composers of jazz and commercial music. An easy way to co struct the modes is to think of them as either a major or minor scale with alterations, or as a major sca beginning and ending on a pitch other than the tonic.

The Church Modes

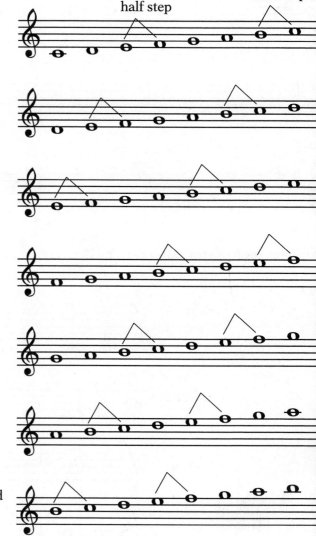

Ionian (major)

Dorian—a minor scale with a raised 6th or a major scale played from the supertonic to the supertonic

Phrygian—a minor scale with a lowered 2nd or a major scale played from the mediant to the mediant

Lydian—a major scale with a raised 4th or a major scale played from the subdominant to the subdominant

Mixolydian—a major scale with a lowered 7th or a major scale played from the dominant to the dominant

Aeolian (minor)

Locrian (very rare)—a minor scale with a lowered 2nd and 5th or a major scale played from the leading tone to the leading tone

Each mode may be transposed to any of the remaining half steps within the octave, and a circle of fifths can be established for each by following the same rules that apply to the major and minor scales. For example, the Dorian mode with no sharps or flats is called D Dorian. A fifth ascending is A Dorian, with the key signature of one sharp; a fifth descending is G Dorian, with the key signature of one flat. The modes may also be transposed by understanding and memorizing the tetrachord pattern for each (see 3e).

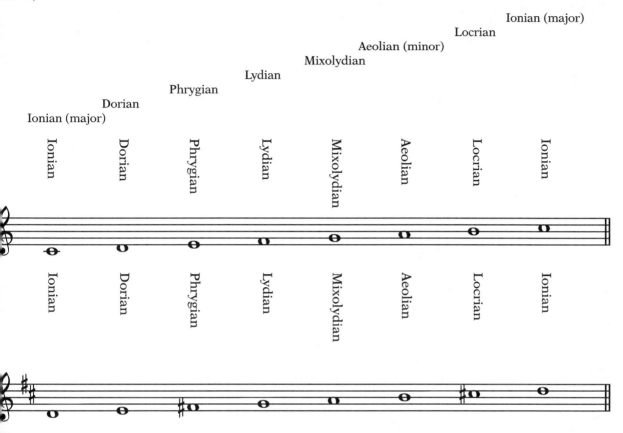

3p OTHER SCALE FORMS

Many other forms of scales can be found in music, including Near Eastern and Asian scales that do not use the half-step and whole-step patterns, scales unique to an ethnic or regional group, and original or "created" scales that are created by the composer for a specific effect.

1) THE PENTATONIC SCALE

The pentatonic scale is a scale with only five different pitches (in contrast to the seven pitches of the major and minor scales). Although there are many ways to construct a pentatonic scale, it can be easily played on the piano by using the black keys only. This scale occurred in China as early as 2000 B.C.

pentatonic scale

(2) THE WHOLE-TONE SCALE

The whole-tone scale, a six-tone scale beginning on C, can be transposed only once, to C♯. All oth[e] transpositions duplicate one of the two scales. This scale was exploited by the French Impression[i] composers of the late nineteenth century because it lacks a feeling of tonic; it thus creates a vaguene[ss] of tonality or key.

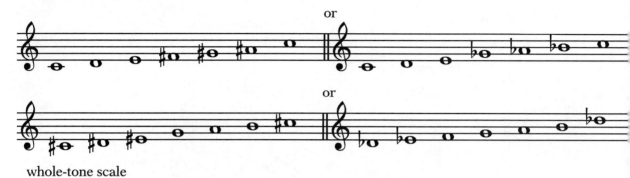

whole-tone scale

(3) THE BLUES SCALE

The blues scale is used frequently in popular music, rock and roll and, of course, the "blues." Since it [is] based on improvisatory practice, there are many different versions of this scale, two of which are show[n] below.

blues scale

blues scale (variant)

(4) ORIGINAL SCALES

A composer may create an original scale for a particular composition. The following is but one of man[y] possible "synthetic" scales.

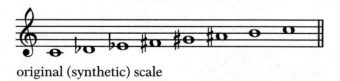

original (synthetic) scale

3q TWELVE-TONE ROWS

In the early twentieth century, the composer Arnold Schoenberg (1874–1951) devised a pitch system to replace the traditional melodic, tonal, and chordal relationships of the music of the eighteenth and nineteenth centuries. A composition using this system is based on an arrangement of all twelve chromatic tones into a series, or **twelve-tone row.** The series usually remains unaltered throughout a work except for the modifications listed below. The composing of a series and its creative use is an advanced and complex skill, but the basic rules can be understood by the beginning theory student:

The row can be used in four forms:
O—in the original form
I—in inversion (upside down, with each interval inverted)
R—in retrograde (backward)
RI—in retrograde inversion (backward and upside down)
These four forms can be transposed to any step of the chromatic scale, allowing a possible total of 48 versions of the original row.
From this basic material, melodic progressions and chordal combinations can be formed. The twelve tones are usually presented in full, arranged horizontally or vertically, before the series, in any of its forms, is repeated.
Any range, clef, skip, repetition of tones, simultaneous use of tones, octave position of tones, or enharmonic spelling of tones is allowed. *Accidentals apply only to the note following.*
Once the row is started, the preestablished note sequence is followed through all the twelve notes of the row. You do not randomly pick notes from the row.

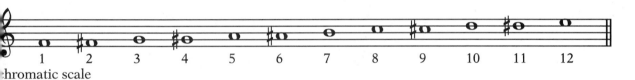

chromatic scale

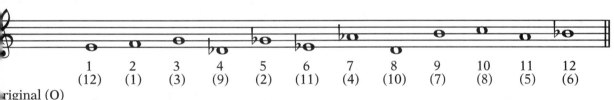

original (O)
the chromatic scale reordered into a twelve-tone row

inversion (I)

retrograde (R)

retrograde inversion (RI)

Here is part of a melody using the inverted form of the row.

This is the row Arnold Schoenberg (1874–1951) used in the following example.

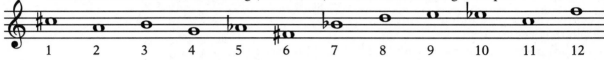

SCHOENBERG, WALTZ, OP. 23, NO. 5

Arrange the twelve chromatic tones in your own twelve-tone row, then construct its remaining thre
forms.

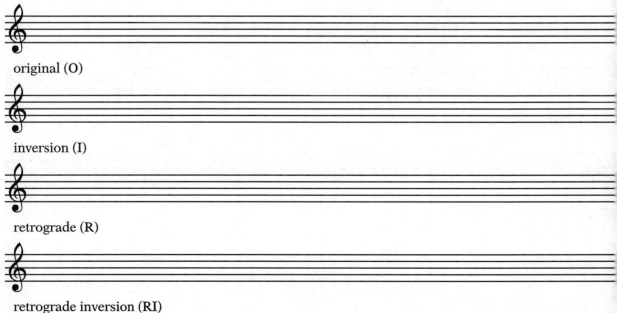

original (O)

inversion (I)

retrograde (R)

retrograde inversion (RI)

Name the major key and write the tonic on the staff for the following key signatures. If possible without ledger lines, write the tonic in two different octaves.

Example

Write the key signatures for the following major keys.

Example   B♭   F♯   G♭

C♯

F   C   C♭

A♭

D♭   A   G

E♭

A   D   B

3d
3f
3g

Write the key signatures for the following major keys.

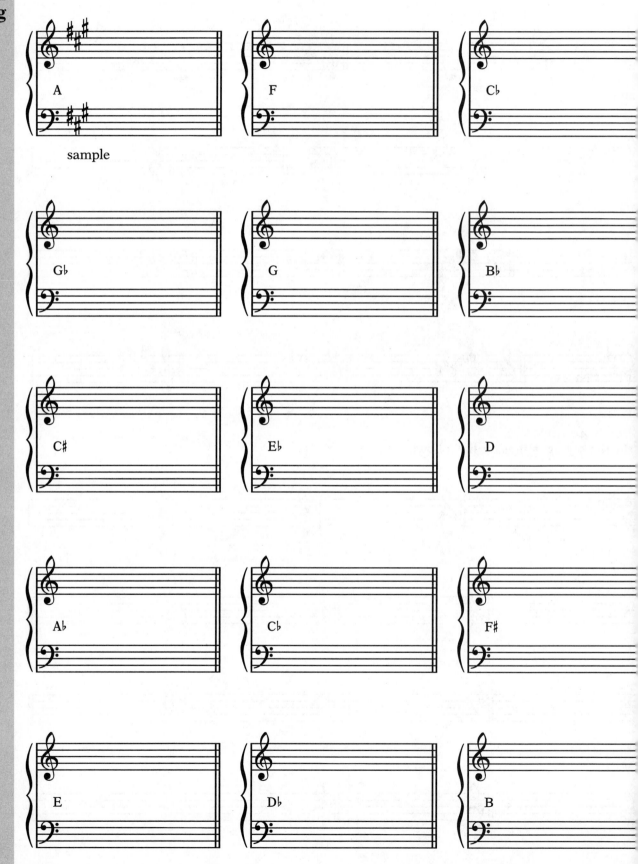

Write the key signatures and the ascending scales for the following major keys.

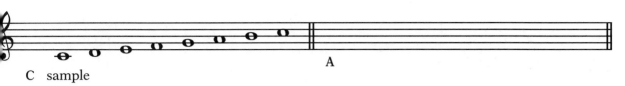

C   sample   A

D♭   G

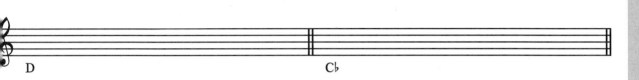

D   C♭

F   A

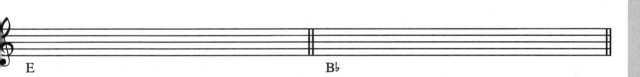

E   B♭

E♭   B

F♯   A♭

E   C♯

G♭   E♭

3d
3e
3f

Identify the key and then write in the key signature for the following *major key* examples.

G   sample

*Modal example. See pp. 96–97.

Name the minor key and write the tonic on the staff for the following key signatures. If possible without ledger lines, write the tonic in two different octaves.

3i
3j

c# sample

Write the key signatures for the following minor keys.

3d
3i
3j

d# sample   g   b   ab

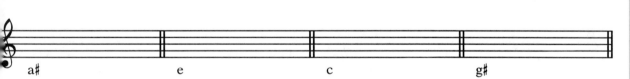

a#   e   c   g#

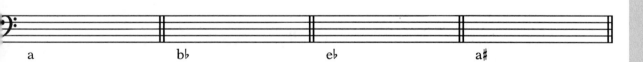

a   bb   eb   a#

d   c#   f   f#

105

NAME _____

3i
3j   Write the key signatures and the ascending scales for the following minor keys. Use the natural form.
3k

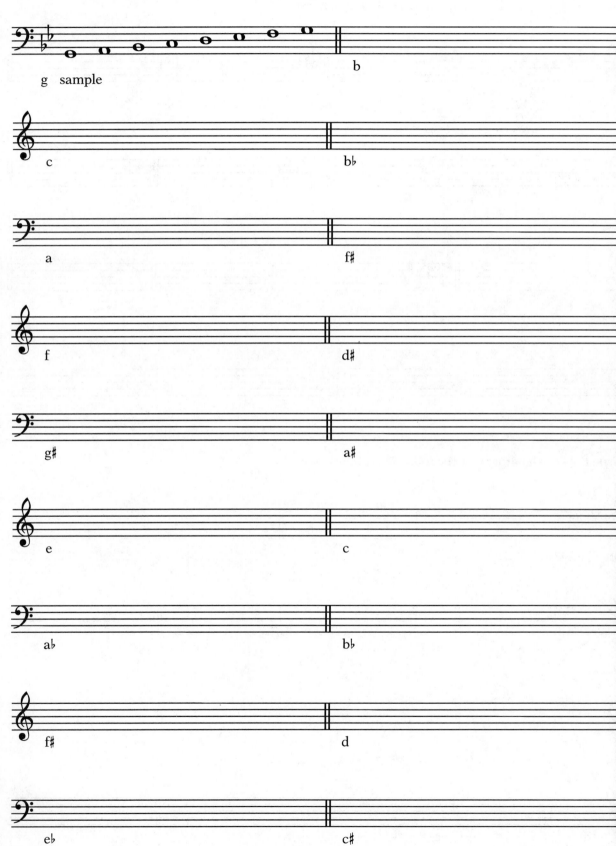

g   sample   b

c   b♭

a   f♯

f   d♯

g♯   a♯

e   c

a♭   b♭

f♯   d

e♭   c♯

Identify the key, *plus the form,* for the following *minor key* examples. Also, write the correct key signature at the beginning of each example.

d natural minor   sample

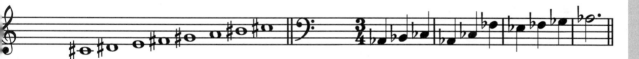

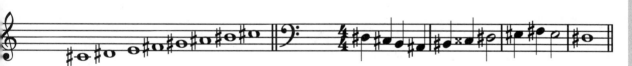

Modal example. See pp. 96–97

3i
3j
3k
3l

Write the ascending *relative* minor scales for the following ascending major scales in all forms indicated

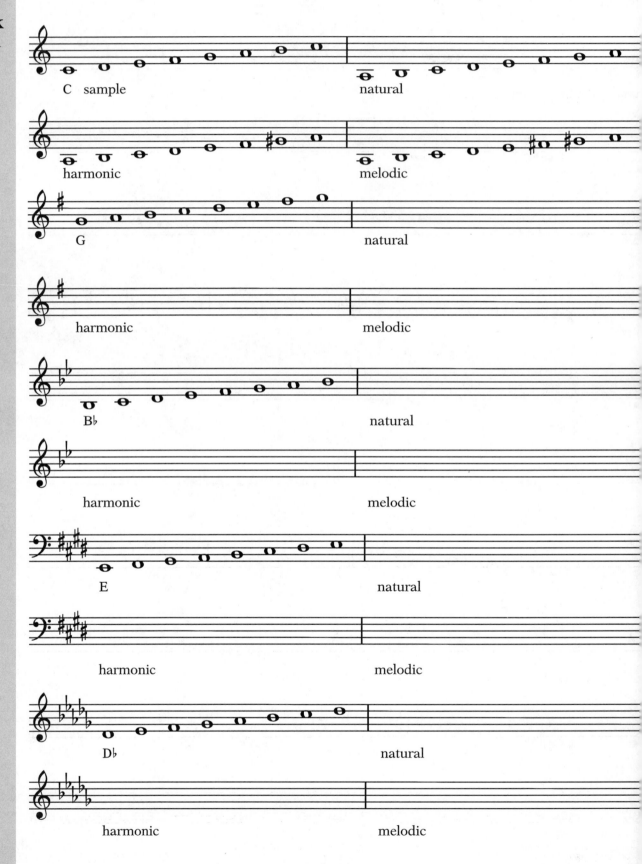

Write the descending *relative* minor scales for the following descending major scales in all forms indicated.

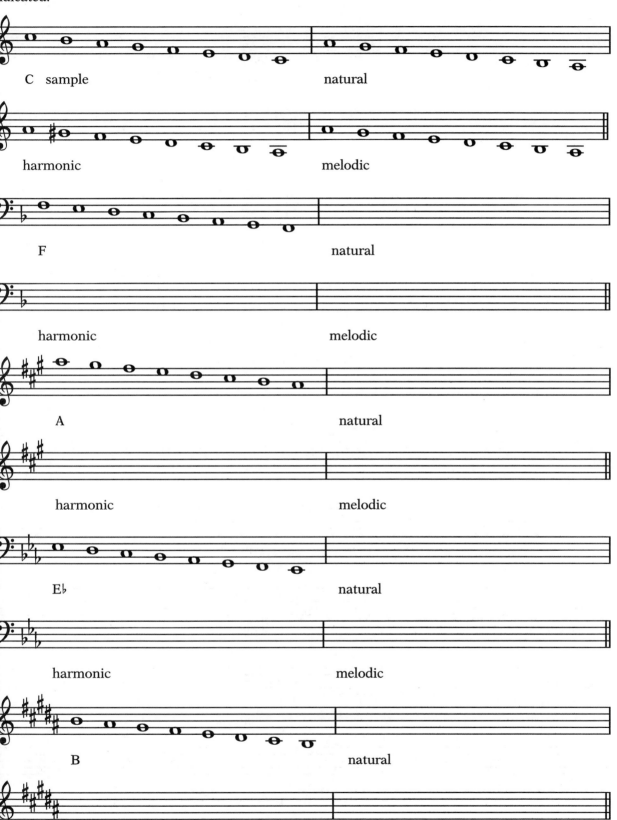

C   sample   natural

harmonic   melodic

F   natural

harmonic   melodic

A   natural

harmonic   melodic

E♭   natural

harmonic   melodic

B   natural

harmonic   melodic

3i
3j
3k
3m

Using the proper key signatures, write the ascending *parallel* minor scales for the following major scale in all forms as indicated.

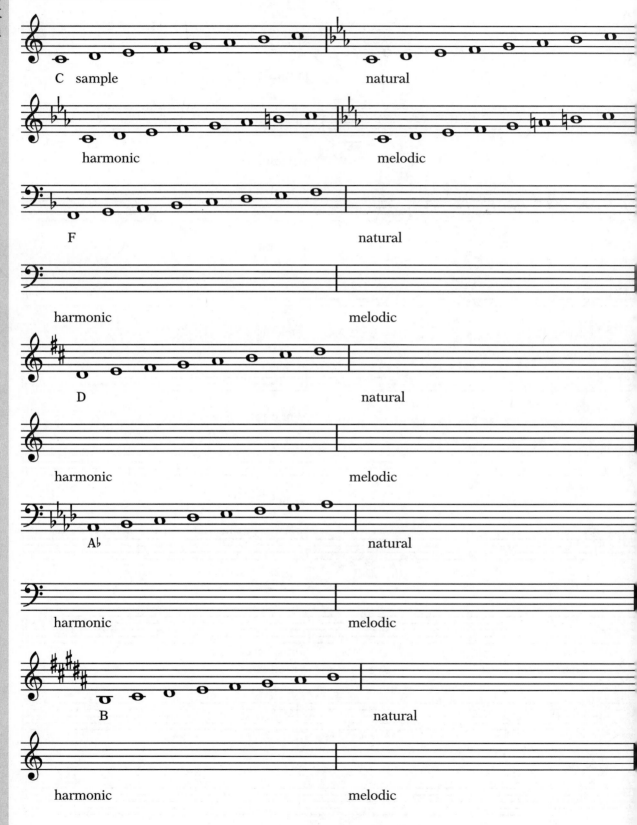

Using the proper key signatures, write the descending *parallel* minor scales for the following major scales in all forms indicated.

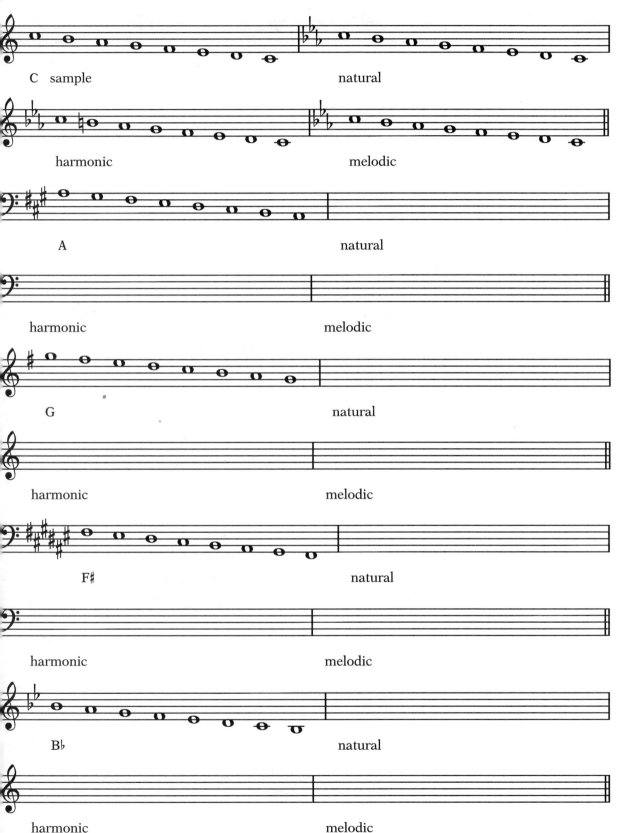

C sample   natural

harmonic   melodic

A   natural

harmonic   melodic

G   natural

harmonic   melodic

F♯   natural

harmonic   melodic

B♭   natural

harmonic   melodic

3k
3l
3m

Write key signatures and *ascending* scales as indicated. For minor scales, use the harmonic form.

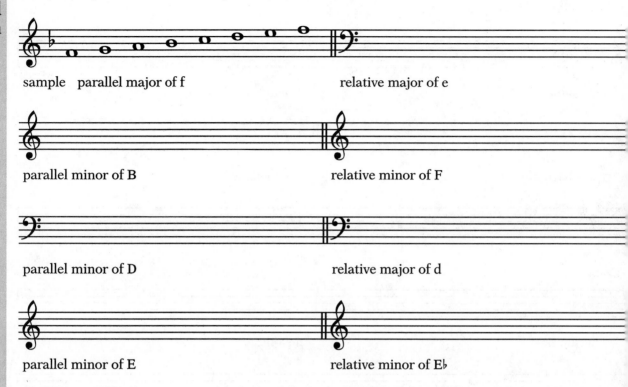

sample   parallel major of f   relative major of e

parallel minor of B   relative minor of F

parallel minor of D   relative major of d

parallel minor of E   relative minor of E♭

Write key signatures and *descending* scales as indicated. For minor scales, use the melodic form.

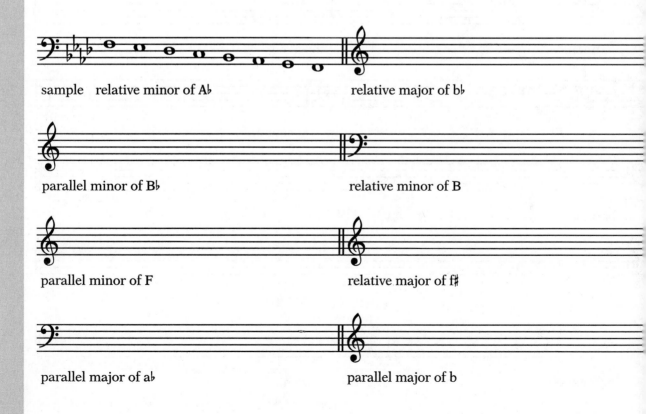

sample   relative minor of A♭   relative major of b♭

parallel minor of B♭   relative minor of B

parallel minor of F   relative major of f♯

parallel major of a♭   parallel major of b

WORKSHEET 3-13   NAME _____

Write key signatures and *ascending* scales as indicated.

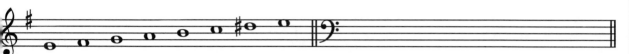

sample   parallel minor (harmonic) of E   relative major of c

relative minor (natural) of A   relative minor (harmonic) of D

parallel minor (melodic) of D   parallel minor (melodic) of C♯

parallel minor (natural) of A   relative major of f

Write key signatures and *descending* scales as indicated.

sample   relative major of f♯   parallel minor (harmonic) of B♭

relative minor (melodic) of E♭   parallel major of g

relative major of a♯   parallel major of g♭

relative minor (harmonic) of C♭   parallel major of b♭

3k
3l
3m
3n
3o

Write key signatures and *ascending* scales as indicated.

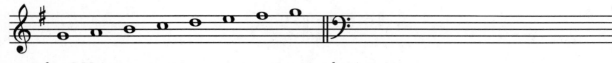

sample   G Major   b minor

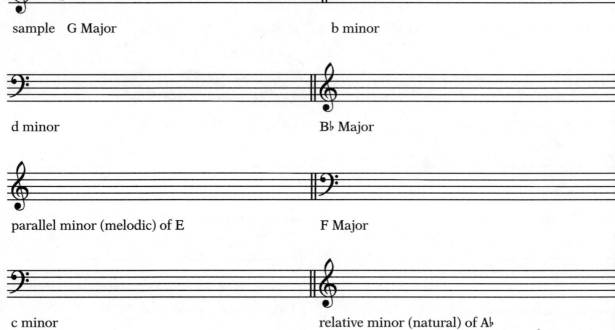

d minor   Bb Major

parallel minor (melodic) of E   F Major

c minor   relative minor (natural) of Ab

Write key signatures and *descending* scales as indicated.

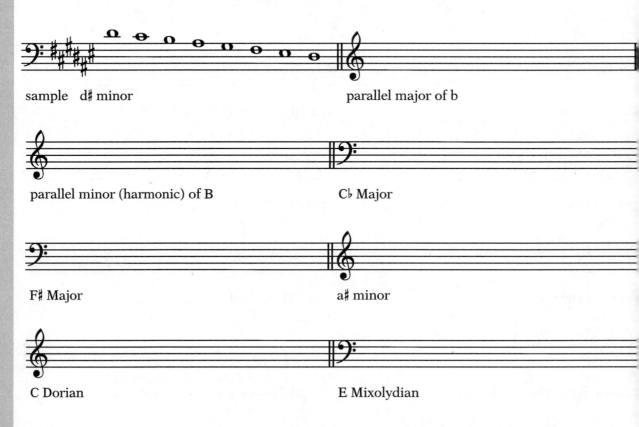

sample   d# minor   parallel major of b

parallel minor (harmonic) of B   Cb Major

F# Major   a# minor

C Dorian   E Mixolydian

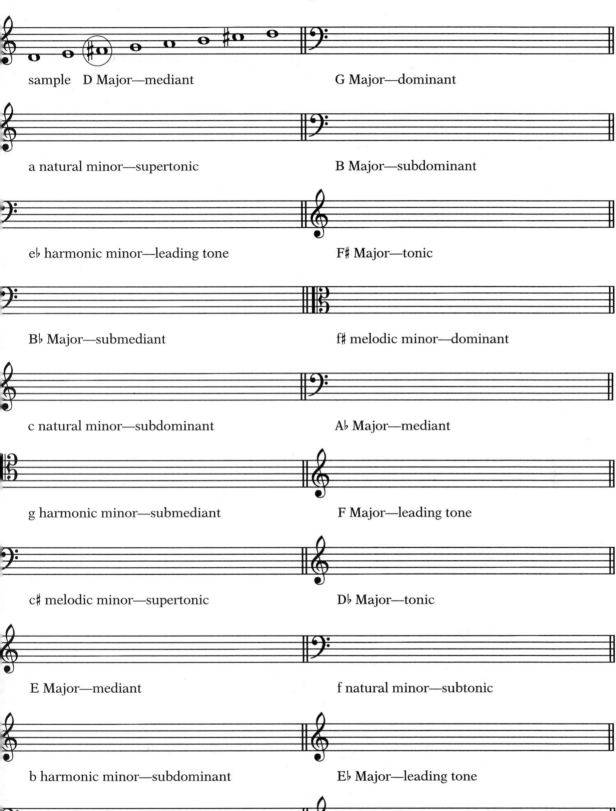

Write the scale indicated and then circle the scale degree indicated.

sample   D Major—mediant

G Major—dominant

a natural minor—supertonic

B Major—subdominant

e♭ harmonic minor—leading tone

F♯ Major—tonic

B♭ Major—submediant

f♯ melodic minor—dominant

c natural minor—subdominant

A♭ Major—mediant

g harmonic minor—submediant

F Major—leading tone

c♯ melodic minor—supertonic

D♭ Major—tonic

E Major—mediant

f natural minor—subtonic

b harmonic minor—subdominant

E♭ Major—leading tone

a♯ melodic minor—submediant

G♭ Major—dominant

1. Name the major key and write the tonic on the staff for the following key signatures.

3f
3g

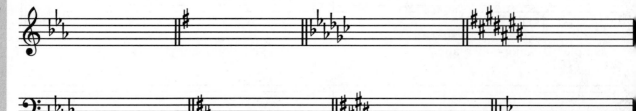

2. Write the key signatures for the following major keys.

3d
3f
3g

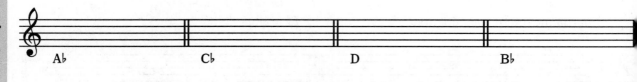

Ab   Cb   D   Bb

B   F#   F   G

3. Write the key signature and the ascending scale for the following major keys.

3d
3f
3d

F   A

Db   F#

4. Name the minor key and write the tonic on the staff for the following key signatures.

3i
3j

5. Write the key signatures for the following minor keys.

3d
3i
3j

g♯   a♭   f   b

d   c   f♯   a

6. Write the key signature and the *ascending* scale for the following minor keys. Use the melodic form.

3i
3j
3k

f♯   g

b♭   d♯

7. Write key signatures and *descending* scales as indicated. Use the harmonic form.

3k
3l
3m

parallel minor of C♯   relative minor of D♭

8. Write key signatures and *ascending* scales as indicated. Use the melodic form.

relative minor of G   parallel minor of F

9. Write key signatures and *ascending* scales as indicated.

3o

E Dorian   F Mixolydian

0. Write an *ascending* and *descending* chromatic scale from A to A. Note the key signature.

3n

4a CONSTRUCTING INTERVALS

n **interval** is the distance between two tones. All intervals have two components—*number size* and *uality*. The number size of an interval is calculated by counting the total number of letter names etween and including the two tones, either up or down, as in the examples below. **Be sure to count ne starting note as "one" when calculating an interval.**

to D includes only two degrees of the staff, C and D, so the interval is a :cond.

to D (counting down) includes three letters of the alphabet, F, E, and , so the interval is a third.

to G includes seven degrees of the staff, so the interval is a seventh.

The quality of an interval is its distinctive sound. The interval of a second, for example, always ncludes two tones, but it is the number of half steps or whole steps between the two that dictates its uality. C-D♭♭, C-D♭, C-D, C-D♯, and C-D𝄪 are all diatonic seconds, but each sounds different—each has s own unique quality.

4b PERFECT AND MAJOR INTERVALS

Vithin a major diatonic scale, there are four perfect and four major intervals above the tonic of that :ale. In the following examples, the perfect and major intervals are named from C or A, the root (tonic) ı the scales of C or A major. In identifying the perfect and major intervals in other major keys, be sure › keep in mind the sharps or flats in the key signature.

The perfect intervals are the unison, fourth, fifth, and octave and are called "perfect" because the are overtones that are closely connected to the fundamental tone (see 3c). Although the unison—*perfe prime*—cannot be counted by a total of letter names between the two tones, it is nevertheless an interva

The major intervals are the second, third, sixth, and seventh. *Major* means "larger," as opposed t *minor*, which means "smaller."

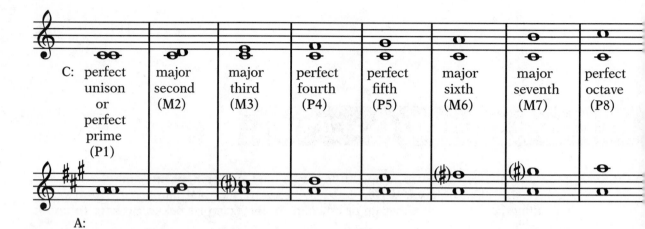

4c MINOR INTERVALS

A major interval made one half step smaller becomes a **minor** interval. The top tone is lowered one half step, or the bottom tone is raised one half step. Changing minor to major is the reverse.

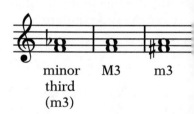

In the unaltered natural minor scale (3k) there are four perfect, three minor, and one major interva above the tonic of the scale. In the following examples, the perfect, minor, and major intervals ar named from C or A, the root (tonic) in the scales of c and a minor.

4d DIMINISHED AND AUGMENTED INTERVALS

minor interval made one half step smaller becomes diminished. The top tone is lowered one half step or the bottom tone ised one half step.

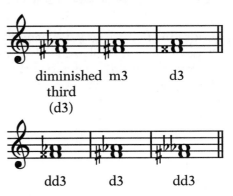

diminished m3   d3
third
(d3)

Rare) A diminished interval made one half step smaller becomes doubly diminished. The top tone is lowered one half step or the bottom tone raised one half step.

dd3   d3   dd3

perfect interval made one half step smaller becomes diminished. The top tone is lowered one half step or the bottom tone ised one half step.

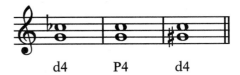

d4   P4   d4

perfect interval or major interval made one half step larger ecomes augmented. The top tone is raised one half step or the ottom tone lowered one half step.

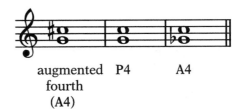

augmented P4   A4
fourth
(A4)

*P = Perfect
M = Major
m = minor
d = diminished
A = Augmented

Half steps	+1	+2	-1	-2
P	A	AA	d	dd
M	A	AA	m	d

Perfect Intervals	Major Intervals
1, 4, 5, 8	**2, 3, 6, 7**
d ← P → A	**d ← m ← M → A**

A perfect interval made one half step *larger* is augmented.

A major interval made one half step *larger* is augmented.

A perfect interval made one half step *smaller* is diminished.

A major interval made one half step *smaller* is minor.

A major interval made two half steps *smaller* is diminished.

4e CONSTRUCTING INTERVALS—BY HALF STEPS AND WHOLE STEPS

Besides the number of letter names between the two tones, intervals can be identified and constructed by the number of whole and half steps they encompass. For the major second and third, and for the perfect fourth and fifth, memorize the number of whole and half steps above or below a given tone, as shown below. For the major sixth and seventh, memorize the number of whole and half steps *less than an octave* that each contains. For example, an octave above C is C; one diatonic half step below C is B. *Make sure you think diatonic*. So B is a major seventh above C. Or an octave *below* C is C; one diatonic half step above that C is Db, a major seventh below C. Again, it is important that you think *diatonic*. Once you identify the major or perfect interval, you can alter it to minor, diminished, or augmented by the methods described in sections 4c and 4d.

In this method of interval construction, write an interval, first observing the correct degrees of the staff. Then alter, if necessary, being sure of the correct diatonic spelling. For example, a major third above D (D-E-F) is F♯, not G♭ (D-E-F-G is a fourth).

unison

M2
one whole step
(two half steps)

M3
two whole steps
(four half steps)

P4
two whole and one half steps

P5
three whole and one half steps

M6
one whole and one half steps *less* than an octave

M7
one half step *less* than an octave

P8
octave

Intervals in Order of Half Steps

Intervals	Half Steps	Whole Steps
Unison – Perfect Prime	0	0
dim 2	0	0
Aug Prime	1	½
m 2	1	½
M 2	2	1
dim 3	2	1
Aug 2	3	1½
m 3	3	1½
M 3	4	2
dim 4	4	2
Aug 3	5	2½
P 4	5	2½
Aug 4	6	3
dim 5	6	3
P 5	7	3½
dim 6	7	3½
Aug 5	8	4
m 6	8	4
M 6	9	4½
dim 7	9	4½
Aug 6	10	5
m 7	10	5
M 7	11	5½
dim 8	11	5½
Aug 7	12	6
P 8	12	6
Aug 8	13	6½

or
Less than an octave

	Half Steps	Whole Steps
dim 6	5	2½
m 6	4	2
M 6	3	1½
dim 7	3	1½
Aug 6	2	1
m 7	2	1
M 7	1	½
dim 8	1	½
Aug 7	0	0
P 8	0	0

Intervals in Order of Names

Intervals	Half Steps	Whole Steps
Unison – Perfect Prime	0	0
Aug Prime	1	½
M 2	**2**	**1**
m 2	1	½
dim 2	0	0
Aug 2	3	1½
M 3	**4**	**2**
m 3	3	1½
dim 3	2	1
Aug 3	5	2½
P 4	**5**	**2½**
dim 4	4	2
Aug 4	6	3
P 5	**7**	**3½**
dim 5	6	3
Aug 5	8	4
M 6	**9**	**4½**
m 6	8	4
dim 6	7	3½
Aug 6	10	5
M 7	**11**	**5½**
m 7	10	5
dim 7	9	4½
Aug 7	12	6
P 8	**12**	**6**
dim 8	11	5½
Aug 8	13	6½

or
Less than an octave

	Half Steps	Whole Steps
M 6	**3**	**1½**
m 6	4	2
dim 6	5	2½
Aug 6	2	1
M 7	**1**	**½**
m 7	2	1
dim 7	3	1½
Aug 7	0	0
P 8	**0**	**0**
dim 8	1	½

4f CONSTRUCTING INTERVALS DOWNWARD

There are three methods of constructing an interval below a given tone, all of which apply to compound as well as simple intervals:

1. by identification and alteration
2. by counting whole steps and half steps (already described in section 4e)
3. by interval inversion

(1) METHOD IDENTIFICATION AND ALTERATION

Count down the correct number of letter names without considering accidentals. Then from the bottom tone identify the quality of the interval and, if necessary, alter the bottom tone to produce the desired interval. (Remember: *lowering* the bottom tone makes an interval larger; *raising* the bottom tone makes an interval smaller.)

For example: what is a major sixth below C? E is the sixth pitch below C. E-C is identified from the bottom tone as a minor sixth. Therefore, the E must be altered *down* by a half step to E♭. The interval is now a major sixth.

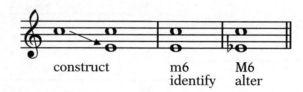

(2) METHOD COUNTING BY WHOLE AND HALF STEPS

See section 4e for a description of this method.

For example: what is a major sixth below E? It is four whole steps plus one half step below.

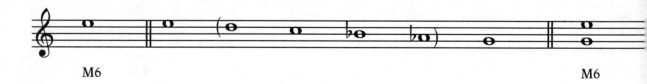

3) METHOD BY INTERVAL INVERSION

you are at ease finding intervals above a note you may find intervals below a given note by following a
w simple rules. (1) Remember that an *inverted* interval adds up to *nine*—a third above C is E and a
xth below C is E. (2) In inversion the quality of the interval changes from major ↔ minor, augmented
↔ diminished, and perfect ↔ perfect. For example, what is a minor third below A? A major sixth *above*
is F♯; therefore, a minor third *below* A is also F♯.

An interval and its inversion will always add up to *nine*.

A second inverted is a seventh.	A fifth inverted is a fourth.
A third inverted is a sixth.	A sixth inverted is a third.
A fourth inverted is a fifth.	A seventh inverted is a second.

The quality of an interval will change when it is inverted, with the exception of the perfect intervals.

P ←————————————————→ **P**
A perfect interval inverted remains perfect.

M ←————————————————→ **m**
A major interval inverted is minor and
a minor interval inverted is major.

A ←————————————————→ **d**
An augmented interval inverted is diminished and
a diminished interval inverted is augmented.

AA ←————————————————→ **dd**
A doubly augmented interval inverted is doubly diminished and
a doubly diminished interval is doubly augmented.

nversion of Intervals

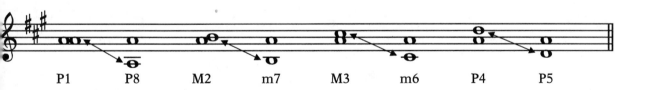

P1   P8   M2   m7   M3   m6   P4   P5

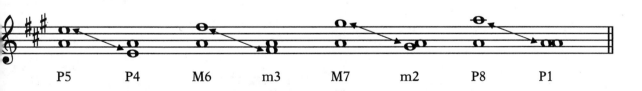

P5   P4   M6   m3   M7   m2   P8   P1

4g THE TRITONE

When all the fourths of the major scale are arranged in order, the one built on the fourth degree of the scale is one half step larger than a perfect fourth; therefore, it is augmented. The augmented fourth contains *three whole steps,* so it is called the **tritone,** meaning "three tones." In a melodic progression, the tritone sounds awkward. In early music it was forbidden, and was referred to as "the devil in music." In certain contexts, including student work, the rule prohibiting the melodic tritone is still observed.

4h SIMPLE AND COMPOUND INTERVALS

A simple interval is an interval of less than an octave. A compound interval is an interval of an octave or greater. It is easier and more convenient to reduce the compound interval to a simple interval plus an octave. Subtract seven from the compound number and it will give you a quick simple interval equivalent.

> 7 from 10 is a third; a third plus an octave equals a 10th.
> 7 from 12 is a fifth; a fifth plus an octave equals a 12th.

The terms major and perfect also apply to the compound intervals. An 11th is a 4th plus an octave and is called a perfect 11th. A 13th is a 6th plus an octave and is called a major 13th.

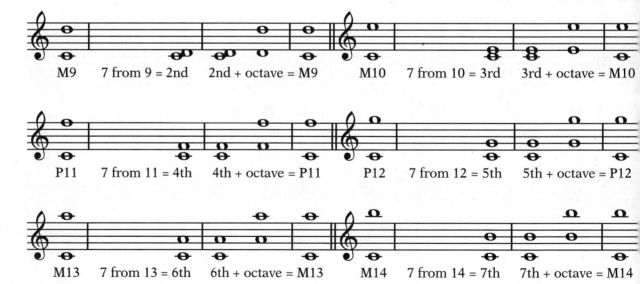

M9	7 from 9 = 2nd	2nd + octave = M9	M10	7 from 10 = 3rd	3rd + octave = M10
P11	7 from 11 = 4th	4th + octave = P11	P12	7 from 12 = 5th	5th + octave = P12
M13	7 from 13 = 6th	6th + octave = M13	M14	7 from 14 = 7th	7th + octave = M14

Compound Intervals in Order of Names

M 9 m 9 d 9 A 9	**P 8 + M 2** P 8 + m 2 P 8 + d 2 P 8 + A 2
M 10 m 10 d 10 A 10	**P 8 + M 3** P 8 + m 3 P 8 + d 3 P 8 + A 3
P 11 d 11 A 11	**P 8 + P 4** P 8 + d 4 P 8 + A 4
P 12 d 12 A 12	**P 8 + P 5** P 8 + d 5 P 8 + A 5
M 13 m 13 d 13 A 13	**P 8 + M 6** P 8 + m 6 P 8 + d 6 P 8 + A 6
M 14 m 14 d 14 A 14	**P 8 + M 7** P 8 + m 7 P 8 + d 7 P 8 + A 7
P 15 d 15 A 15	**P 8 + P 8** P 8 + d 8 P 8 + A 8

4b   Complete the following by adding major seconds *above* the given notes.*

*Notation of the second requires the notes to touch, the higher note to the right. Accidentals are placed in front of both notes, following the same pattern as the notes; the lower accidental to the left and the upper accidental to the right.

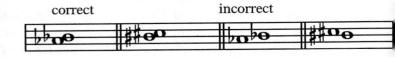

correct   incorrect

sample

Complete the following by adding major thirds *above* the given notes.

sample

Complete the following by adding perfect fourths *above* the given notes. Notice that all perfect fourths are ♮-♮, ♯-♯, or ♭-♭, except for F to B♭ and F♯ to B.

rule   exception

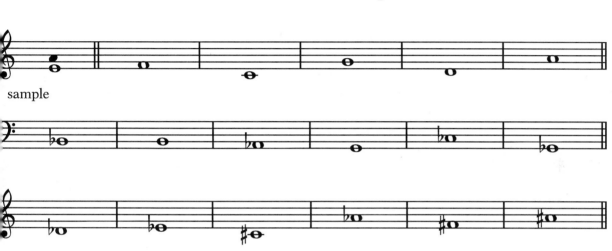

sample

4b Complete the following by adding perfect fifths *above* the given notes. Notice that all perfect fifths a♮
♮-♮, ♯-♯, or ♭-♭, except for B to F♯ and B♭ to F.

rule   exception

sample

Complete the following by adding a major sixth *above* the given notes.

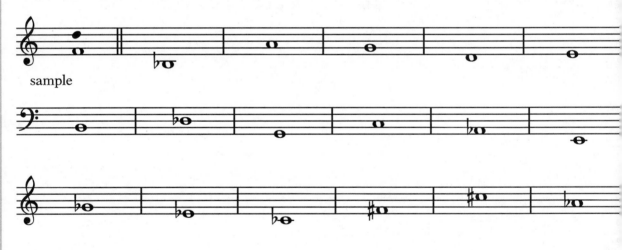

sample

Complete the following by adding a major seventh *above* the given notes.

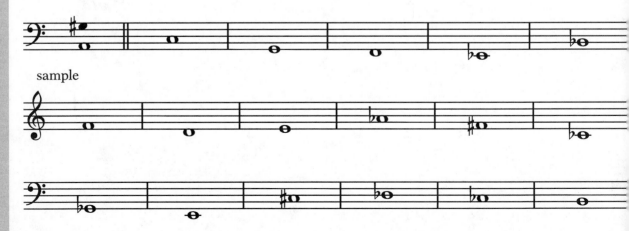

sample

130

Complete the following intervals by adding a note *above* the given note.

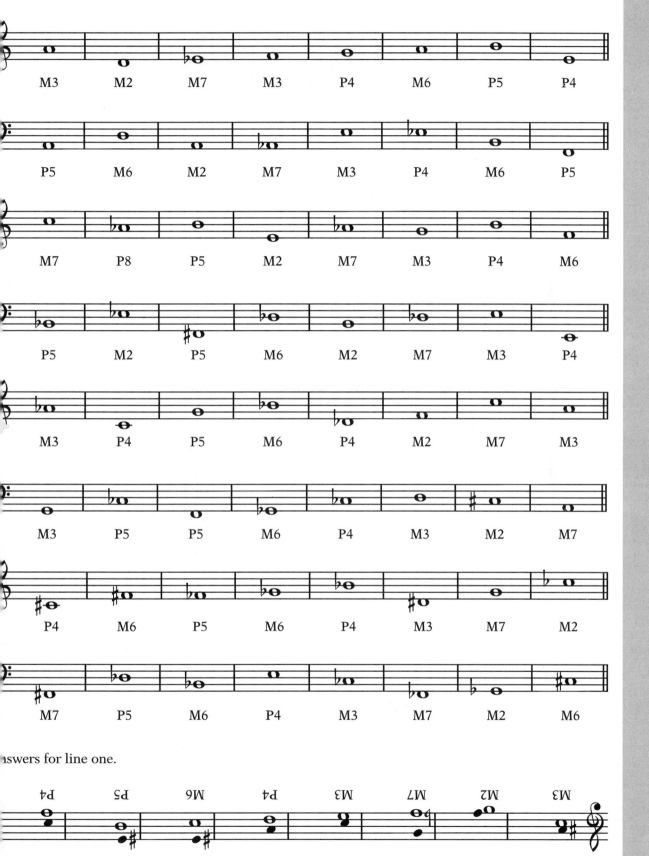

M3   M2   M7   M3   P4   M6   P5   P4

P5   M6   M2   M7   M3   P4   M6   P5

M7   P8   P5   M2   M7   M3   P4   M6

P5   M2   P5   M6   M2   M7   M3   P4

M3   P4   P5   M6   P4   M2   M7   M3

M3   P5   P5   M6   P4   M3   M2   M7

P4   M6   P5   M6   P4   M3   M7   M2

M7   P5   M6   P4   M3   M7   M2   M6

Answers for line one.

M3   M2   M7   M3   P4   M6   P5   P4

4b
4c
4d

Complete the following intervals by adding a note *above* the given note.

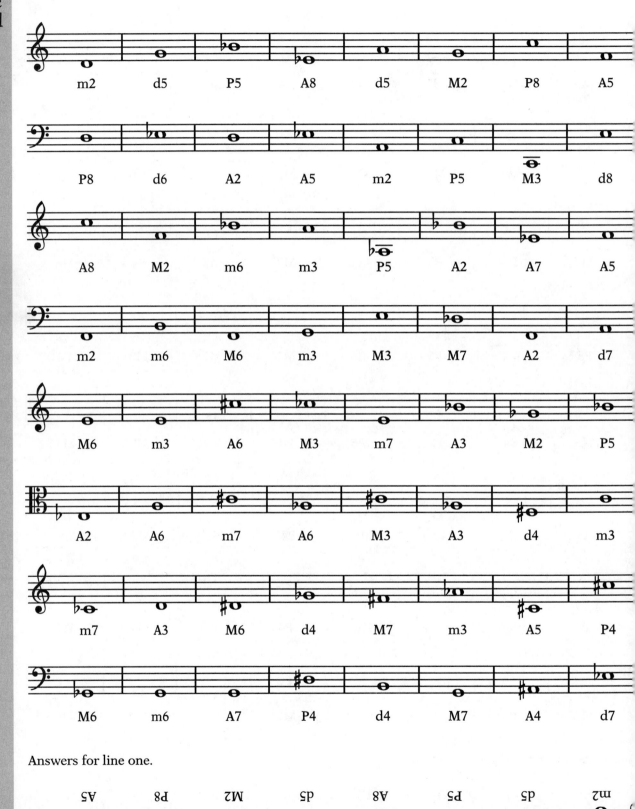

Answers for line one.

NAME _____

Identify the following intervals by number and quality using the abbreviations P, M, m, d, or A.

Example: M2

4b
4c
4d
4h

Identify the following intervals by number and quality using the abbreviations P, M, m, d, or A.

sample: P4

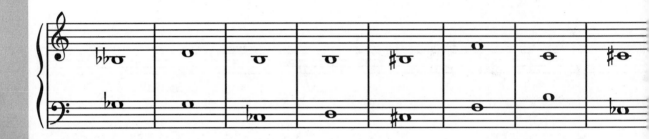

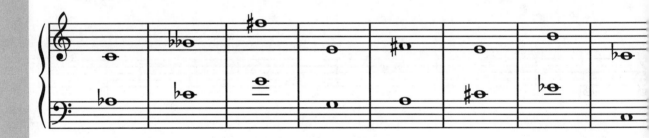

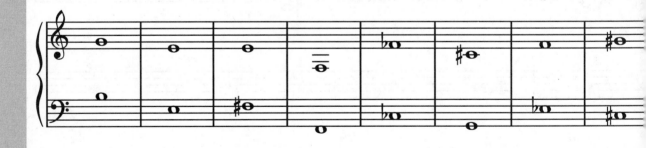

Complete the following by adding major seconds *below* the given notes.

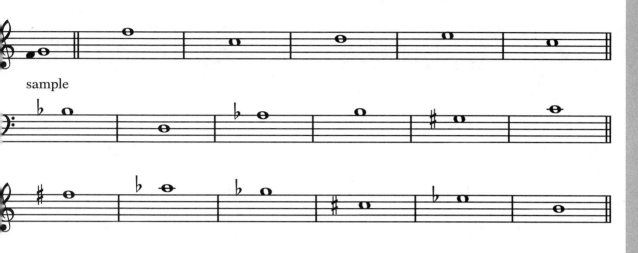

sample

Complete the following by adding a major third *below* the given note.

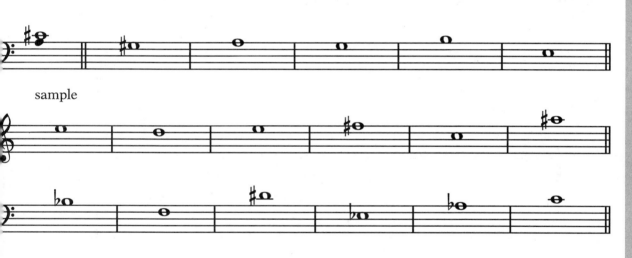

sample

Complete the following by adding a perfect fourth *below* the given note. Notice that all perfect fourths are ♮-♮, ♯-♯, or ♭-♭, except for B♭ to F and B to F♯.

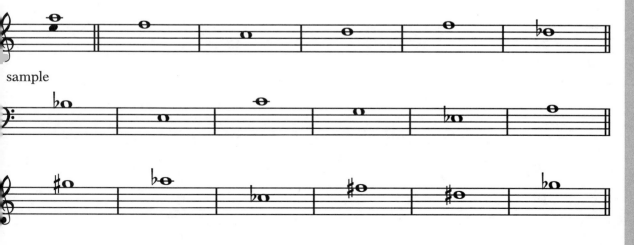

sample

4f Complete the following by adding perfect fifths *below* the given notes. Notice that all perfect fifths ar
♮-♮, ♯-♯, or ♭-♭, except for F to B♭ and F♯ to B.

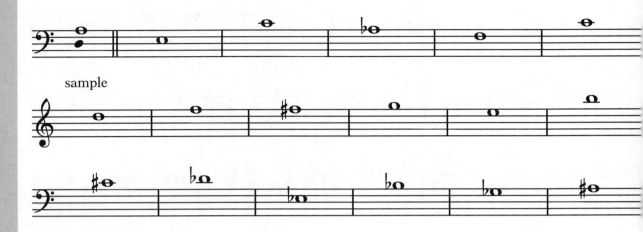

sample

Complete the following by adding a major sixth *below* the given note.

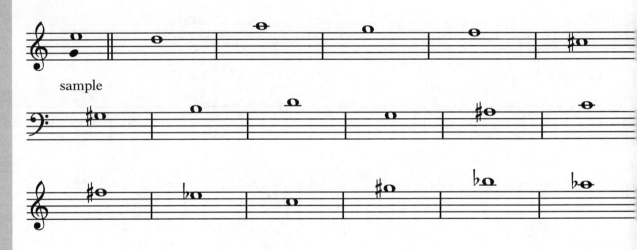

sample

Complete the following by adding a major seventh *below* the given note.

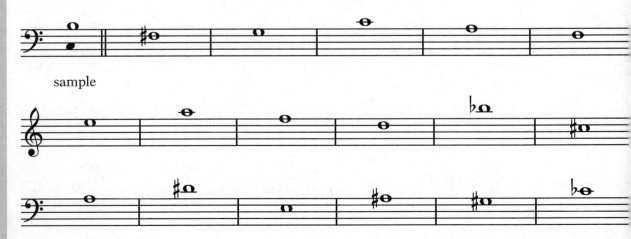

sample

Complete the following intervals by adding a note *below* the given note.

Answers for line one.

WORKSHEET 4-10   NAME _____

4f   Complete the following intervals by adding a note *below* the given note.

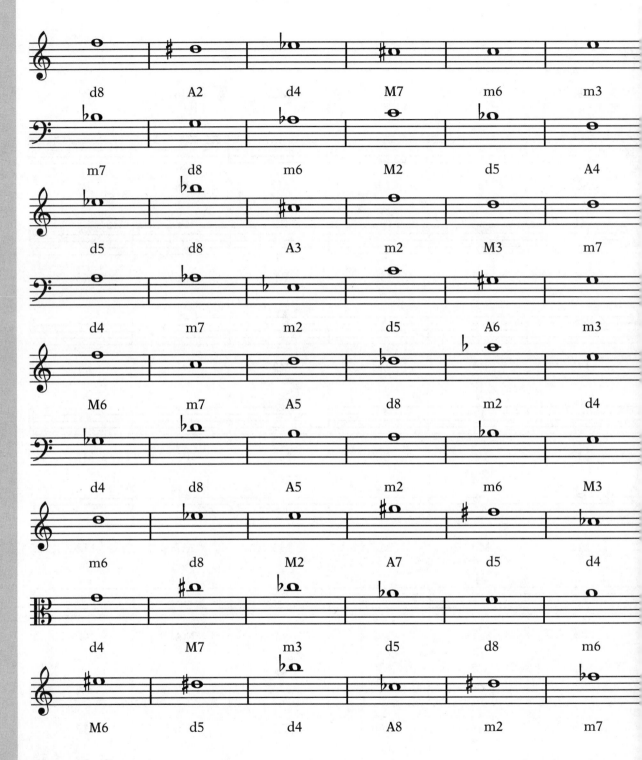

Answers for line one.

NAME _____

Identify the first interval, invert the interval, then identify the inversion.

P4   P5
sample

Identify the interval, then invert the interval by placing the bottom note of the interval above.

sample P5   P4

4h Complete the following compound intervals by adding a note *above* the given note.

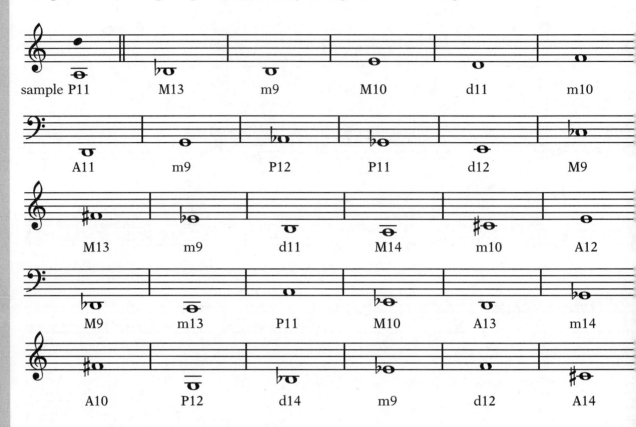

sample P11   M13   m9   M10   d11   m10

A11   m9   P12   P11   d12   M9

M13   m9   d11   M14   m10   A12

M9   m13   P11   M10   A13   m14

A10   P12   d14   m9   d12   A14

Complete the following compound intervals by adding a note *below* the given note.

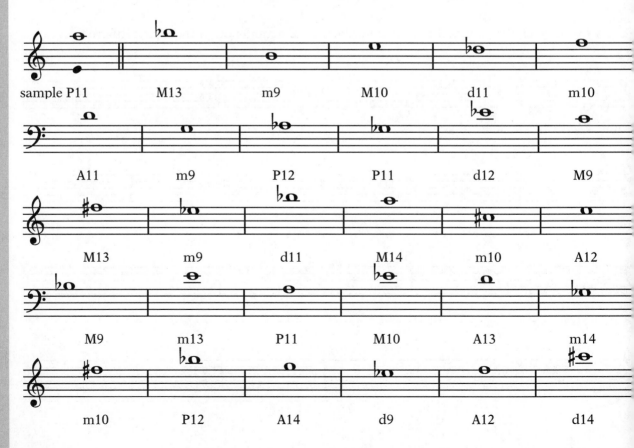

sample P11   M13   m9   M10   d11   m10

A11   m9   P12   P11   d12   M9

M13   m9   d11   M14   m10   A12

M9   m13   P11   M10   A13   m14

m10   P12   A14   d9   A12   d14

Complete the following intervals by adding a note *above* the given note.

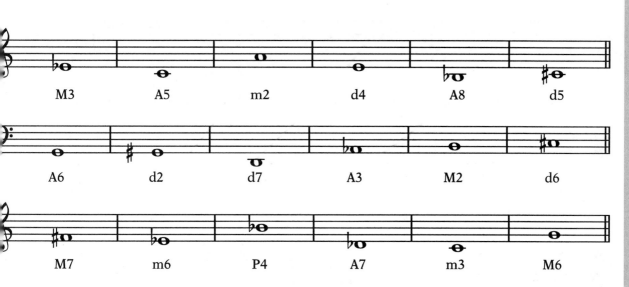

| M3 | A5 | m2 | d4 | A8 | d5 |

| A6 | d2 | d7 | A3 | M2 | d6 |

| M7 | m6 | P4 | A7 | m3 | M6 |

Complete the following intervals by adding a note *below* the given note.

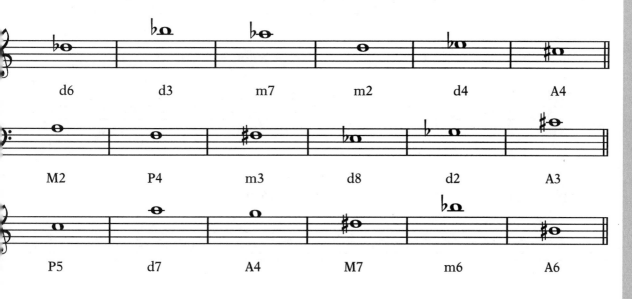

| d6 | d3 | m7 | m2 | d4 | A4 |

| M2 | P4 | m3 | d8 | d2 | A3 |

| P5 | d7 | A4 | M7 | m6 | A6 |

Identify the following intervals by number and quality using the abbreviations P, M, m, d, or A.

4f
(3)

4. Identify the interval, then invert the interval by placing the top note of the interval below.

5. Identify the interval, then invert the interval by placing the bottom note of the interval above.

4b
4c
4d

6. Identify the following intervals by number and quality using the abbreviations P, M, m, d, or A.

4h

7. Complete the following compound intervals by adding a note *above* the given note.

A10   d12   d9   A14   M10   A11

4f
4h

8. Complete the following compound intervals by adding a note *below* the given note.

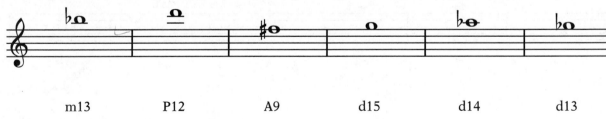

m13   P12   A9   d15   d14   d13

4h

9. Identify the following intervals by number and quality using the abbreviations P, M, m, d, or A.

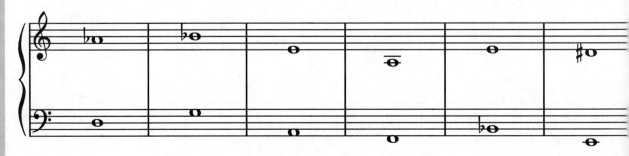

Rhythmic and Melodic
Exercises—Intermediate

Before performing the rhythmic exercises in this unit, review the rules of good practice habits (2a); review also compound meter signatures (1g3). Compound meters involve rhythmic groupings of three beats or divisions of a beat into three equal parts, and may be counted in either of the following ways: count the division values as *1* 2 3, *4* 5 6 (*7* 8 9, *10* 11 12) with an accent on 1, 4 (7, 10); or let the sounds "eh" and "ah" represent the second and third division of each group of three—*1*-eh-ah, *2*-eh-ah *3*-eh-ah, *4*-eh-ah). Both methods have their advantages. Try each method several times and use the one that feels best.

Compound meter signatures convey the feeling of skipping, or of a waltz (*1* 2 3, *1* 2 3), or of a word or words (*pine*apple, *ri*verboat, *Lud*wig van *Bee*thoven). Try to develop a feeling for each meter signature and its characteristic divisions and subdivisions. A simple word pattern or familiar tune may be very helpful in establishing that unique feeling for a particular meter.

5a RHYTHMIC EXERCISES

1) COMPOUND METERS WITH BEAT DIVISION

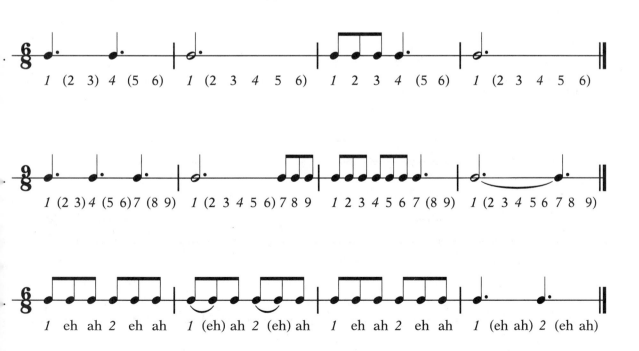

1 eh ah 2 eh ah   1 (eh) ah 2 (eh) ah   1 eh ah 2 eh ah   1 eh ah 2 (eh ah)

2) EIGHT-MEASURE EXERCISES

Review page 32.

Fine

D.C. al Fine

(3) COORDINATED-SKILL EXERCISES

Fine

D.C. al Fine

(4) NEW MATERIAL—DOTTED NOTES ♪. AND ♪.

For an accurate performance of the dotted eighth and sixteenth (♪. ♪ or ♪♪), and the dotted sixteenth and 32nd (♪. ♪ or ♪♪), count the subdivision of the beat, tapping the note on the appropriate word.

In simple meters **2/4 3/4 4/4** : 1 (eh &) ah

In simple meters **2/8 3/8 4/8** : 1 (eh &) ah   In compound meters **6/8 9/8 12/8** : 1 (2) & 3   4 (5) &

1 & ah 2 & ah

3 (4) &   1 (2) &

5) EIGHT-MEASURE EXERCISES

Fine

D.C. al Fine

5) COORDINATED-SKILL EXERCISES

Fine

D.C. al Fine

7) NEW MATERIAL—$\frac{2}{2}$, $\frac{3}{2}$, $\frac{4}{2}$

(8) EIGHT-MEASURE EXERCISES

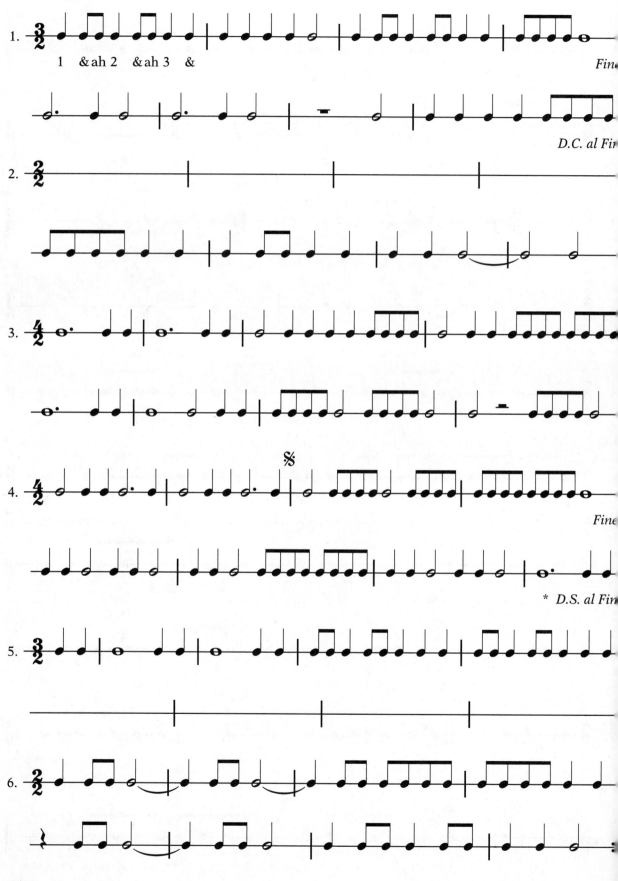

1. 1 & ah 2 & ah 3 &

Fine

D.C. al Fine

2.

3.

4.

Fine

* *D.S. al Fine*

5.

6.

*(1m)

9) NEW MATERIAL—THE TRIPLET

In simple meters, count the triplet 1-eh-ah, 2-eh-ah. Once the triplet division of the beat (three equal notes) has been established, be sure you do not rush or speed up the subdivision (two equal notes) of the beat.

(10) EIGHT-MEASURE EXERCISES

Fine

D.C. al Fin

Fine

D.C. al Fin

Fine

D.S. al Fine

Fine

D.C. al Fine

(11) COORDINATED-SKILL EXERCISES

160

D.S. al coda

Coda

(12) THREE-PART RHYTHMIC EXERCISES

Fin

D.C. al Fin

163

♩ —with foot

5.

164

5b SOLFEGGIO WITH MAJOR KEYS

olfeggio (also called solfège or solmization) is a method of sight singing using the syllables *do-re-mi--sol-la-ti(si)-do*. There are two systems. In the *fixed-do* system, *do* is C, regardless of the key. In the *ovable-do* system, *do* moves according to the key. In the key of E♭, for example, E♭ is *do;* in the key of A is *do*. The movable-*do* system is best for the elementary student in the study of scales and inter-ls while in more advanced study, with the addition of frequent chromatics and key changes, the xed-*do* system offers certain advantages. Both systems are included in the following examples.

The ability to sight-read music is a must for all music students. Not developing this skill will greatly hibit your ability to learn and understand music literature, history, theory, and all other aspects of usic. Solfeggio is an important method in the development of your sight-reading skill.

Sing the following examples by letter names, by numbers (see 2d), and by one of the two solmiza-on methods. Note that *ti* is used in the movable-*do* system and is replaced by *si* in the fixed-*do* system. lso note these pronunciations:

do is pronounced "doe"
fa and *la* are pronounced "fah" and "lah"
re is pronounced "ray"
mi, ti, and *si* are pronounced "mee," "tee," and "see"

5c MELODIC EXERCISES

1) USING SOLFEGGIO SYLLABLES

*(6f)

Review p. 68.

ABA Form, Ternary Form, Song Form

The *D.C. al Fine* creates an ABA (Ternary/Song) form. The opening "A" section is usually repeated. The following "B" section is of contrasting material and in many cases in a different key. The D.C. returns you to the beginning of Section "A" and concludes, without repeat, at the end of the "A" section, therefore it is an AABA form. This form was popular with Classic and Romantic composers and is the most common form for our present-day "pop" ballad.

2) TWO-PART MELODIC EXERCISE

(3) COORDINATED MELODIC-RHYTHMIC EXERCISES

(4) EIGHT-MEASURE EXERCISES

Fine

D.C. al Fine

5) NEW MATERIAL—THE TRIPLET

174

AB Form, Binary Form

The Binary form has two parts. The opening "A" section is repeated and the "B" section is usually repeated. The opening "A" and closing "B" sections may use similar or contrasting material. This form was popular in certain Baroque dance forms and in many early folk tunes. An example of Binary form is "The Star Spangled Banner."

6) TWO-PART MELODIC EXERCISE

(7) COORDINATED MELODIC-RHYTHMIC EXERCISES

5d SOLFEGGIO WITH MINOR KEYS

The fixed-*do* system does not alter any syllable for chromatic alterations. In the movable-*do* system, the chromatic alterations of the diatonic major scale are as shown below. There is no chromatic tone between *mi* and *fa* or between *ti* and *do;* therefore, no altered syllables are necessary.

In the three minor forms, the syllables are altered as shown below.

1) MELODIC EXERCISES

D Major

d minor (melodic)

sol   do   re me re   do   sol sol   le   sol la ti   do   do

le   me   me   le   me   la ti do

(ri)   (fi)

Roman numerals and letters are upper-case for major chords and lower-case for minor chords (6b). For the minor letters, a lower-case *m* or *mi* should be added.

d mi   d mi   A7   d mi

i   i   V7   i

g mi   d mi   A7   d mi

iv   i   V7   i

17. FOUR-PART ROUND (see page 76)

Charles Gounod

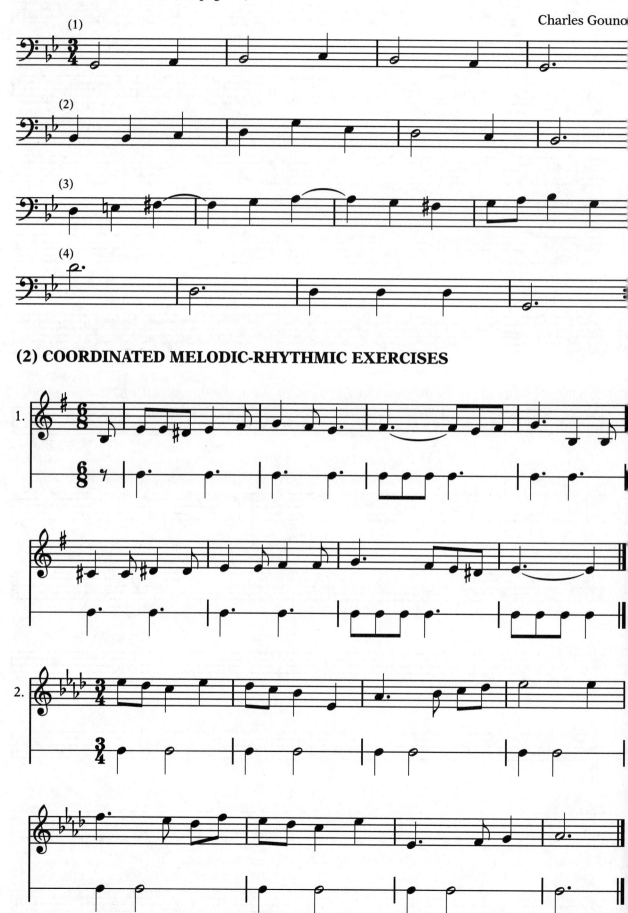

(2) COORDINATED MELODIC-RHYTHMIC EXERCISES

184

186

Unit 6

Chords

A **chord** is several tones (three or more) played at the same time. The most common chord, the kind be discussed in this unit, is constructed of consecutive intervals of the third. Chords can be, and a constructed of intervals other than thirds, the most common being chords of intervals of the four (quartal harmony). You may find it interesting to experiment with the construction and sounds chords of the fourth.

6a TRIADS

A **triad** is a three-tone chord combining a root and the intervals of a third and a fifth above the root. T *root* is the tone from which the chord is both constructed and named. All the chords in the followi examples are F chords in root position (6d).

(1) MAJOR TRIADS

When the quality of the third is major and the quality of the fifth is perfect, the triad is **major.** A maj triad may be constructed from any pitch by building these intervals above a given root. The major tri is the first, third, and fifth of any major scale.

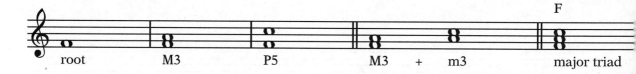

root   M3   P5   M3   +   m3   major triad

(2) MINOR TRIADS

When the quality of the third is minor and the quality of the fifth is perfect, the triad is **minor.** A min triad may be constructed from any pitch by building these intervals above a given root. The minor tri is the first, third, and fifth of any minor scale. It is a major triad with a lowered third.

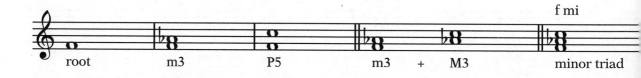

root   m3   P5   m3   +   M3   minor triad

188

3) DIMINISHED TRIADS

When the quality of the third is minor and the quality of the fifth is diminished, the triad is **diminished.** A diminished triad may be constructed from any pitch by building these intervals above a given root. It is a major triad with a lowered third and fifth.

root   m3   d5   m3   +   m3   diminished triad

4) AUGMENTED TRIADS

When the quality of the third is major and the quality of the fifth is augmented, the triad is **augmented.** An augmented triad may be constructed from any pitch by building these intervals above a given root. It is a major triad with a raised fifth.

root   M3   A5   M3   +   M3   augmented triad

6b CHORD NAMES AND SYMBOLS

Each scale step and its corresponding chord have a name that indicates their relationship to the tonic, the name of the main tone of a key.

tonic—the beginning pitch
supertonic—the pitch *above* the tonic
mediant—the pitch halfway between the tonic and the dominant
subdominant—the dominant (five pitches) *below* the tonic
dominant—the fifth pitch *above* the tonic
submediant—the pitch a fifth *below* the mediant
leading tone—half-step below the tonic; the pitch that "leads" back to the tonic
or *subtonic*—whole-step below the tonic; the lowered seventh pitch in natural minor

Roman numerals are used to represent each chord constructed above the pitches of a scale. Capital numerals are used for major chords, lower-case numerals for minor chords, lower-case numerals plus a small circle (°) for diminished chords, and capital numerals plus a small plus sign (+) for augmented chords.

Major scale degrees	Chord symbols	Chord names
1	I	tonic
2	ii	supertonic
3	iii	mediant
4	IV	subdominant
5	V	dominant
6	vi	submediant
7	vii°	"leading tone"

The triads built above the C major scale and their corresponding numbers are shown in the following example.

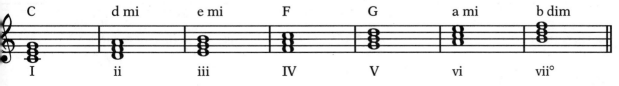

C   d mi   e mi   F   G   a mi   b dim

I   ii   iii   IV   V   vi   vii°

6c PRIMARY TRIADS

The three most important triads are the **primary triads**—those constructed above the first, fourth, a[nd] fifth pitches of the major or minor scale. Those constructed above the second, third, sixth, and seven[th] pitches are called *secondary chords*. The primary triads are the three major triads in the diatonic ma[jor] scale, and they have a particularly close harmonic relationship: the dominant (V) lies a perfect fi[fth] above the tonic, and the subdominant (IV) lies a perfect fifth below the tonic.

The tonic triad (I), constructed on the first scale degree, ranks first in importance. Tonal music[al] compositions (music with a clearly defined key) often begin and almost invariably end on the ton[ic] chord. The dominant triad exercises great harmonic influence, especially with the addition of a seven[th] (see 6f). The dominant chord is second in importance, and the subdominant is third.

Below is a list of the primary triads of all the major scales. Play these triads on the piano until yo[ur] hand and ear are thoroughly familiar with them.

In the *natural* minor form, all of the primary triads are minor (i-iv-v). This is the least used of t[he] minor forms. In the *harmonic* minor form, the tonic and subdominant are minor and the dominant [is] major (i-iv-V). In the ascending *melodic* minor form, the tonic is minor and the subdominant and dom[i]nant are major (i-IV-V). In the descending *melodic* minor form, all of the primary triads are minor (t[he] *natural* minor form i-iv-v).

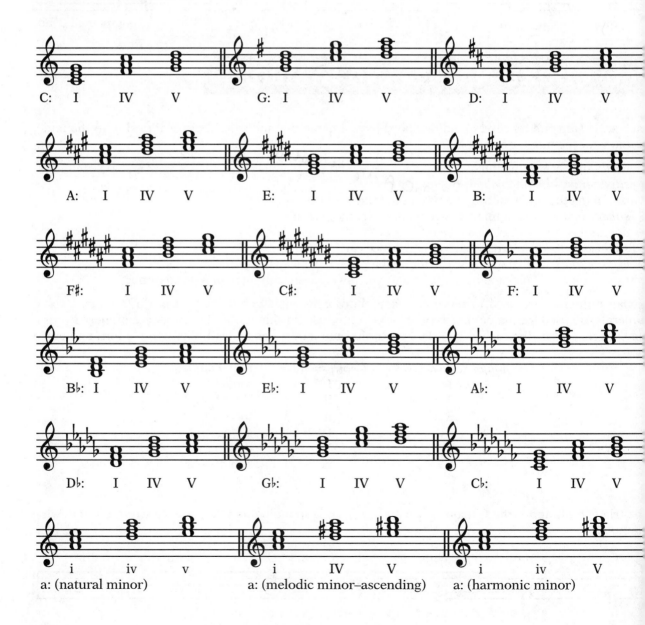

C: I IV V   G: I IV V   D: I IV V

A: I IV V   E: I IV V   B: I IV V

F#: I IV V   C#: I IV V   F: I IV V

Bb: I IV V   Eb: I IV V   Ab: I IV V

Db: I IV V   Gb: I IV V   Cb: I IV V

a: (natural minor)   i iv v   a: (melodic minor–ascending)   i IV V   a: (harmonic minor)   i iv V

6d ROOT POSITION TRIAD TABLE

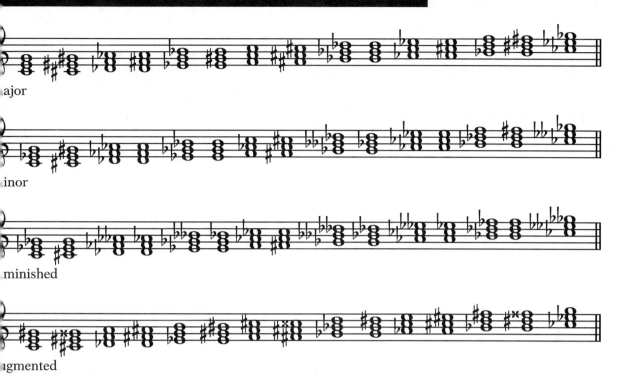

ajor

inor

minished

ugmented

6e ROOT POSITION AND INVERSION

hen the root of a triad is in the bass—that is, when the root is the lowest tone sounded—the triad is in **ot position**. If any other tone is in the bass the triad is **inverted**. If the third of the triad is in the bass, e triad is in **first inversion**; if the fifth is in the bass, the triad is in **second inversion**.

Root-position and inverted C major triads are shown below in two positions—*closed position*, in hich all the notes are within one octave, and *open position*, in which the notes span more than an tave.

ot position—C, on which the C major triad built, is the lowest tone sounded.

rst inversion—E, the third of the triad, is the west tone sounded.

cond inversion—G, the fifth of the triad, is e lowest tone sounded.

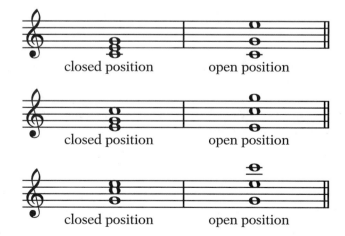

6f SEVENTH CHORDS

A four-tone chord combining a triad and the interval of a seventh above the root is called a **seven[th] chord.** Like all chords, seventh chords can be constructed on any given pitch.

(1) MAJOR SEVENTH CHORDS

When the quality of the triad is major and the quality of the seventh is major, the chord is called a **maj[or] seventh chord.**

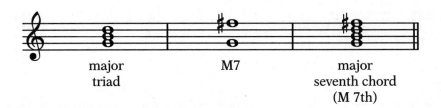

major triad   M7   major seventh chord (M 7th)

(2) MAJOR-MINOR SEVENTH CHORDS— THE DOMINANT SEVENTH CHORD

When the quality of the triad is major and the quality of the seventh is minor, the chord is called [a] **major-minor seventh chord.** Of all the seventh chords, it is the most frequently used.

This chord is called the **dominant seventh chord** when it is built above the *fifth* scale degree. As [we] have seen, the dominant triad (V) is second in importance only to the tonic triad; similarly, the dom[i]nant seventh is harmonically a very important chord.

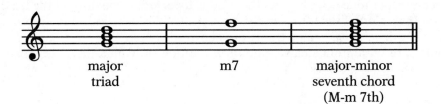

major triad   m7   major-minor seventh chord (M-m 7th)

(3) MINOR SEVENTH CHORDS

When the quality of the triad is minor and the quality of the seventh is minor, the chord is called [a] **minor seventh chord.**

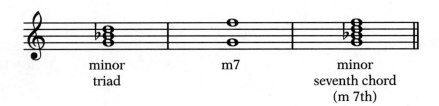

minor triad   m7   minor seventh chord (m 7th)

) HALF-DIMINISHED SEVENTH CHORDS

hen the quality of the triad is diminished and the quality of the seventh is minor, the chord is called a
lf-diminished seventh chord. The half-diminished seventh chord can also be considered a minor
venth chord with its fifth pitch lowered—therefore, a minor seventh, flat five.

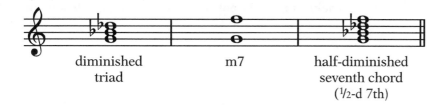

diminished   m7   half-diminished
triad   seventh chord
($^1\!/_2$-d 7th)

) DIMINISHED SEVENTH CHORDS

hen the quality of the triad is diminished and the quality of the seventh is diminished, the chord is
lled a **diminished seventh chord.**

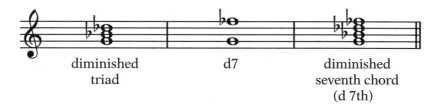

diminished   d7   diminished
triad   seventh chord
(d 7th)

) TABLE OF ROOT-POSITION SEVENTH CHORDS

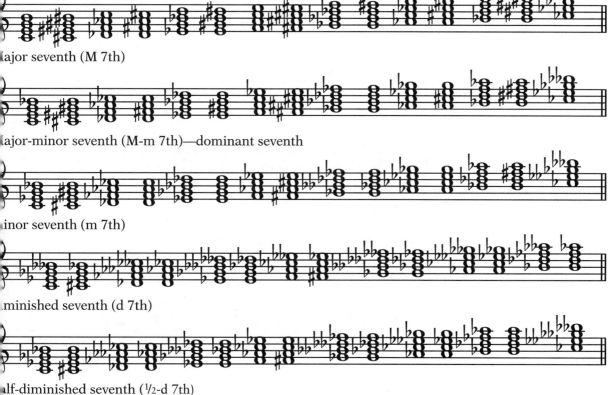

lajor seventh (M 7th)

lajor-minor seventh (M-m 7th)—dominant seventh

inor seventh (m 7th)

minished seventh (d 7th)

alf-diminished seventh ($^1\!/_2$-d 7th)

(7) SEVENTH-CHORD INVERSIONS

When the root of a seventh chord is in the bass—that is, when it is the lowest tone sounded—the seventh chord is in root position. If any other tone is in the bass, the chord is **inverted.** If the third of the seventh chord is in the bass, the chord is in first inversion. If the fifth is in the bass, the chord is in second inversion. If the seventh is in the bass, the chord is in third inversion.

Root-position and inverted major-minor seventh chords are shown below in both closed and open position.

Root position—The tone on which the chord is built is the lowest tone sounded.

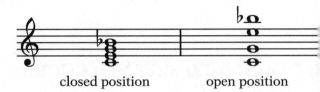

First inversion—The third of the chord is the lowest tone sounded.

Second inversion—The fifth of the chord is the lowest tone sounded.

Third inversion—The seventh of the chord is the lowest tone sounded.

Inversions of closed-position seventh chords will inevitably lead to the interval of the second. According to the general rule, the top note of the second is to the right.

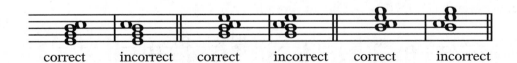

If a stem is added, *all notes must touch the stem,* but the rule of the top note of the second remains.

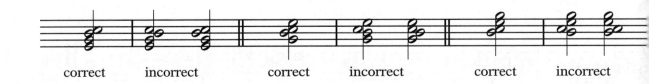

The chord symbols used in commercial music are different from those used in theory classes. The symbols are not completely uniform in all printed commercial music, but the principles are standard. Symbols are always placed above the staff. (For simplicity, all the examples below are notated in C.) Upper-case letters are used for all chords, regardless of their quality.

	Common	Less Common
A capital letter stands for a major triad. When the root is flat or sharp, the flat or sharp is added to the letter name even if it is in the key signature.	C	CM–CMa–CMaj–CΔ
Minor, augmented, and diminished triads, respectively, are indicated by adding one of the following to the letter name: *m, min,* or *mi; +* or *aug; °* or *dim.*	Cm	Cmi–Cmin–C-
	Caug	C+
	Cdim	C°
6 adds a major sixth above the root of a major or minor triad.	C6	CM6–CMa6
	Cm6	Cmin6
The number **7,** by itself, normally implies a major triad with an added minor seventh.	C7	Cdom7
The number **7** preceded by the letters **Ma** normally implies a major triad with an added major seventh.	CMa7	CMaj7–CM7–CΔ7
The number **7** preceded by a lower-case **m** normally implies a minor triad with an added minor seventh.	Cm7	Cmi7–Cmin7–C-7
The number **7** preceded by the letters **dim** normally implies a diminished triad with an added diminished seventh.	Cdim7	C°7–Cd7

Chord Symbol Chart

Please note that there are other ways to notate these seventh chords, and that there are other seven[?] chord forms. This chart illustrates most of the common chords, and their typical symbols, curren[?] used in commercial music.

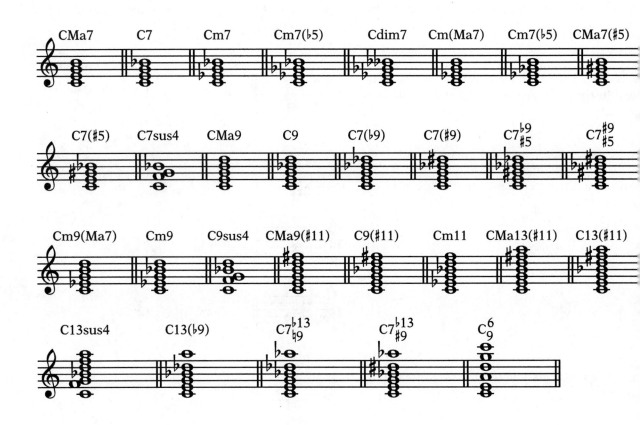

In the study of music theory, the figured bass is used to indicate if a chord is root position or an inve[?] sion. In commercial music, letters are placed above the staff to indicate the desired chord. Inversions [?] the chord are indicated by first the chord letter, a slash mark, and then the desired *root note* (bass no[?] placed below. C over E would be a first inversion, C over G a second inversion.

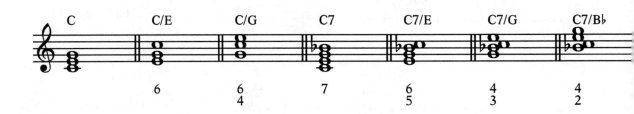

6a Construct the indicated triads *above* the following notes. Please note that a majority of diminish[ed]
triads above *flat notes* will require double flats (♭♭). Augmented chords above a *sharp note* will requir[e]
double sharp (×).

In writing the required accidentals for a given note the accidentals should
be staggered from right to left to right and should not be written in a
straight vertical line. If the two upper notes alone are altered the middle
note accidental appears to the left. If the two lower notes are altered the
lower note accidental appears to the left.

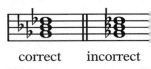

correct   incorrect

Correct order of accidentals

2	1	2	1		
	3			3	2

correct   incorrect   correct   incorrect

M   m   d   A   M   m   d   A
sample

M   m   d   A   M   m   d   A

M   m   d   A   M   m   d   A

M   m   d   A   M   m   d   A

M   m   d   A   M   m   d   A

M   m   d   A   M   m   d   A

M   m   d   A   M   m   d   A

NAME _____

Construct major triads *above* the following notes.

sample

Construct minor triads *above* the following notes.

sample

Construct diminished triads *above* the following notes.

sample

Construct augmented triads *above* the following notes.

sample

6a   Construct the following triad chords using the given note as the *root* of the chord.

Answers for line one.

onstruct major triads using the given note as the *root* of the triad.

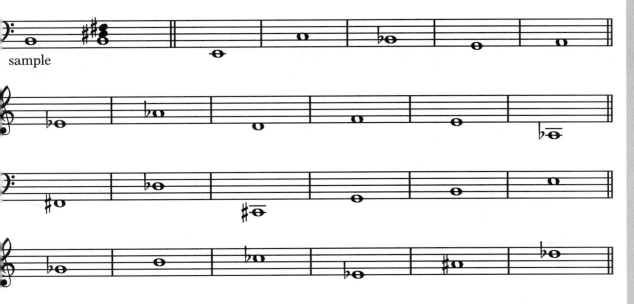

sample

onstruct major triads using the given note as the *third* of the triad.

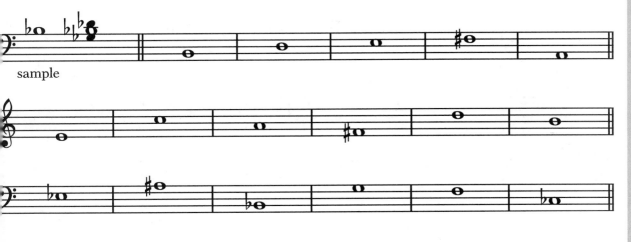

sample

onstruct major triads using the given note as the *fifth* of the triad.

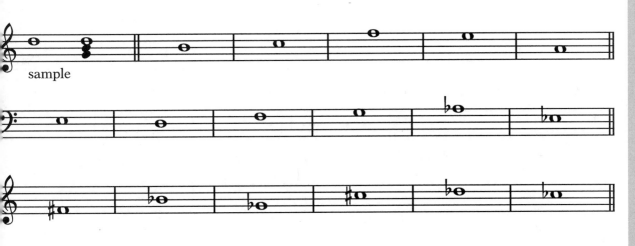

sample

6a
(2)
(3)

Construct minor and diminished triads using the given note as the *root* of the triad.

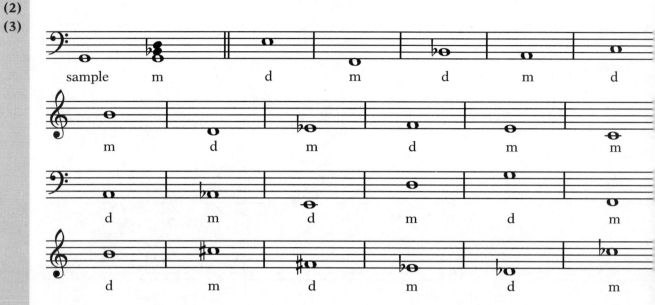

Construct minor and diminished triads using the given note as the *third* of the triad.

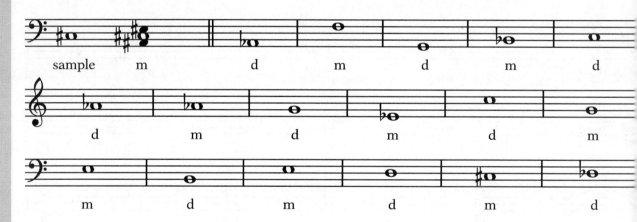

Construct minor and diminished triads using the given note as the *fifth* of the triad.

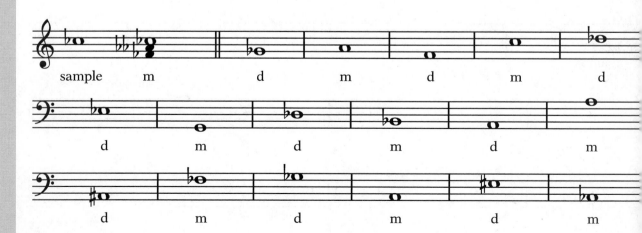

Construct augmented triads using the given note as the *root* of the triad.

sample

Construct augmented triads using the given note as the *third* of the triad.

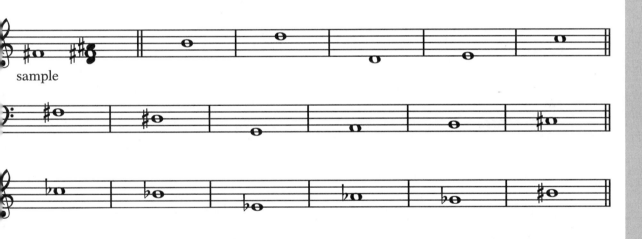

sample

Construct augmented triads using the given note as the *fifth* of the triad.

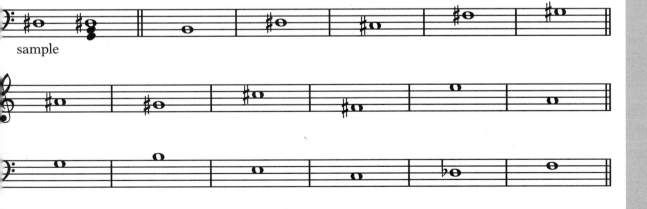

sample

NAME _____

6C Identify the following triads.

Answers for line one.

WORKSHEET 6-8   NAME _____   6d

Identify the inversion of each of the original chords; then reduce them to single closed root-position triads. Identify each chord by name and quality.

sample: 1st inv   FM

Root position   CM
sample

205

6e   Write the three major triads—tonic (I), subdominant (IV), and dominant (V)—in each of the followin[g]
major keys. Label each with the key and the proper Roman numerals.

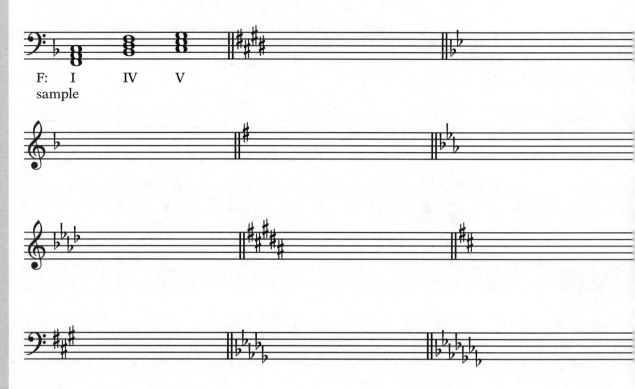

F: I   IV   V
sample

6e   Write the three minor triads and the one diminished triad—supertonic (ii), mediant (iii), submedia[nt]
(vi), and leading tone (vii°)—in each of the following major keys. Label each with the key and the prop[er]
Roman numerals.

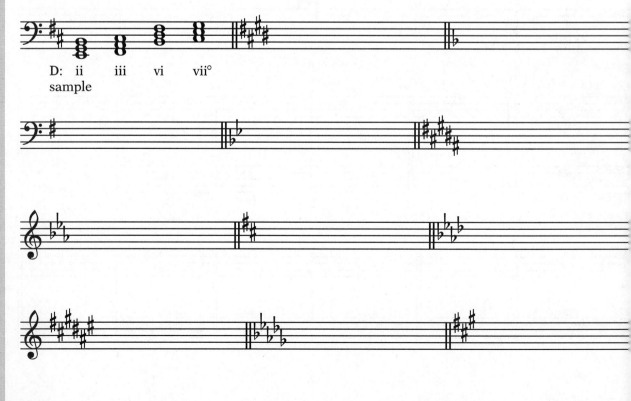

D: ii   iii   vi   vii°
sample

NAME _____

Write the two minor triads—tonic (i) and subdominant (iv)—and the one major triad—dominant (V)—for each of the following *harmonic* minor keys. Label each with the key and the proper Roman numerals.

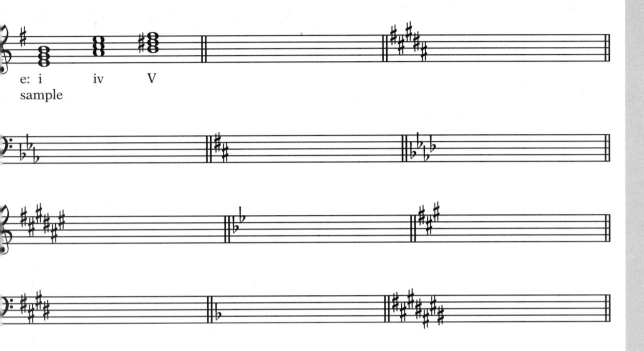

e: i   iv   V
sample

Write the two diminished triads—supertonic (ii°) and leading tone (vii°)—and the augmented triad—mediant (III⁺)—for each of the following *harmonic* minor keys. Label each with the key and the proper Roman numerals.

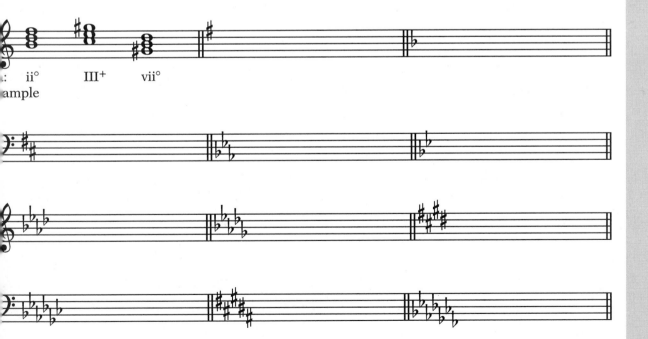

: ii°   III⁺   vii°
ample

NAME _____

6f   Construct the following seventh chords using the given note as the *root* of the chord.

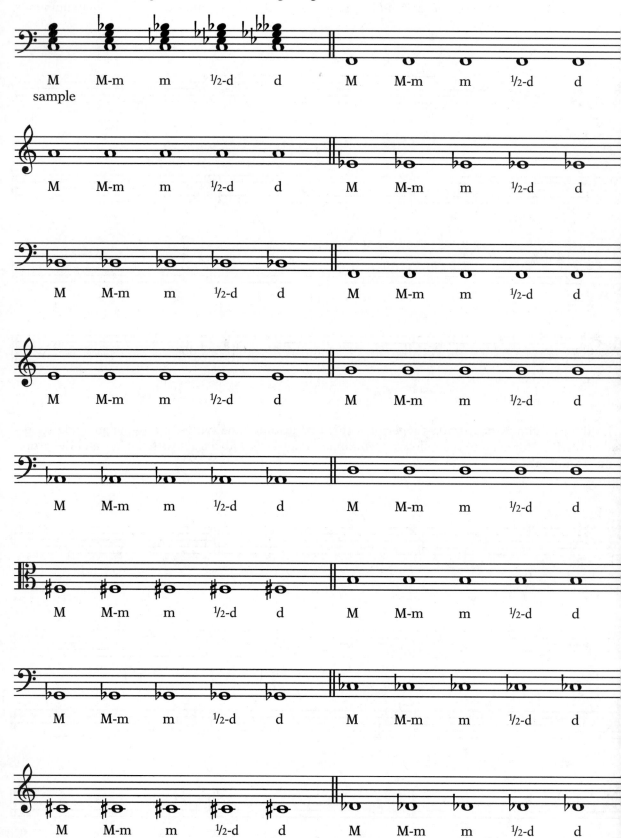

M   M-m   m   ½-d   d   M   M-m   m   ½-d   d

sample

M   M-m   m   ½-d   d   M   M-m   m   ½-d   d

M   M-m   m   ½-d   d   M   M-m   m   ½-d   d

M   M-m   m   ½-d   d   M   M-m   m   ½-d   d

M   M-m   m   ½-d   d   M   M-m   m   ½-d   d

M   M-m   m   ½-d   d   M   M-m   m   ½-d   d

M   M-m   m   ½-d   d   M   M-m   m   ½-d   d

M   M-m   m   ½-d   d   M   M-m   m   ½-d   d

Construct major seventh chords above the following notes.

sample

Construct major-minor seventh chords above the following notes.

sample

NAME _____

6f
(3)
Construct minor seventh chords above the following notes.

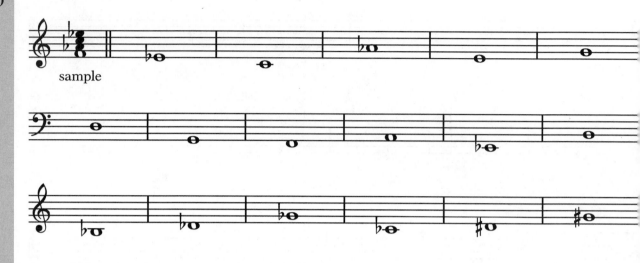

sample

6f
(4)
Construct half-diminished seventh chords above the following notes.

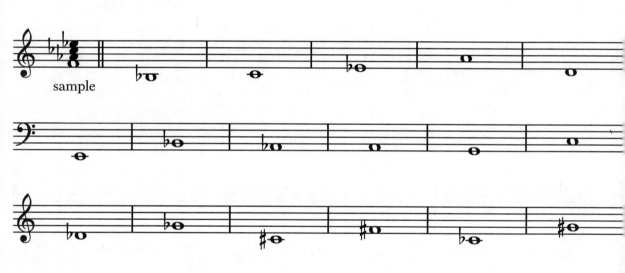

sample

6f
(5)
Construct diminished seventh chords above the following notes.

sample

Construct the following seventh chords using the given note as the *root* of the chord.

6f
(1)
(2)
(3)
(4)
(5)

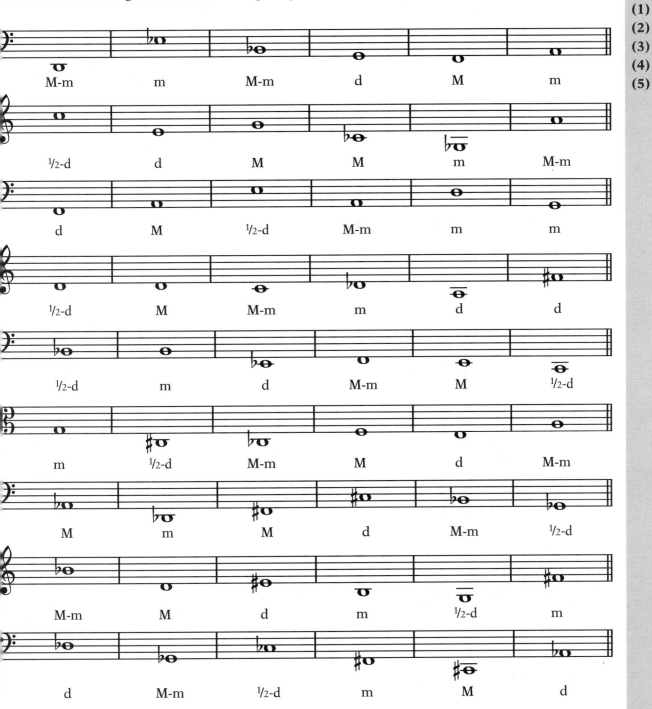

Answers for line one.

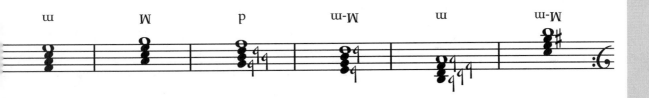

6f
(1)
(2)
(3)
(4)
(5)

Construct the following seventh chords using the given note as the *root* of the chord.

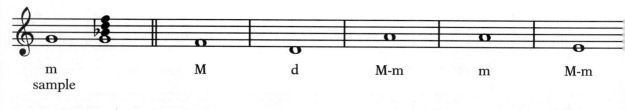

Construct seventh chords using the given note as the *third* of the chord.

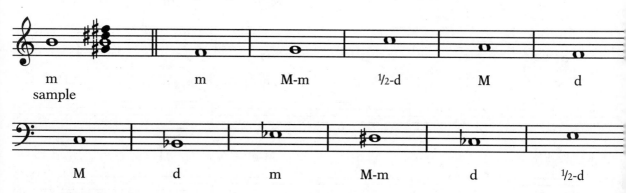

Construct seventh chords using the given note as the *fifth* of the chord.

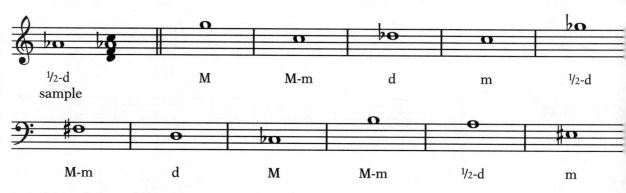

Construct seventh chords using the given note as the *seventh* of the chord.

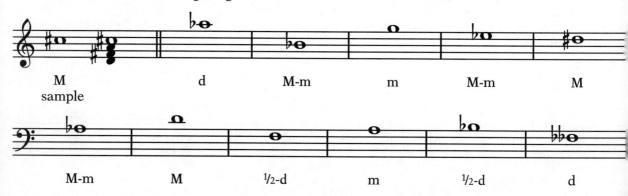

NAME _____

entify the following seventh chords.

nswers for line one.

6f
(7)   Identify the inversion of each of the original chords; then reduce them to single closed root-positi
         chords. Identify each chord by name and quality.

3rd inv   d min 7
sample

1st inv   CM/m7
sample

WORKSHEET 6-18NAME _____

Construct the primary chords—I-IV-V7 for major, i-iv-V7 for harmonic minor, i-iv-v7 for natural minor, and i-IV-V7 for (ascending) melodic minor—for the following major and minor keys.

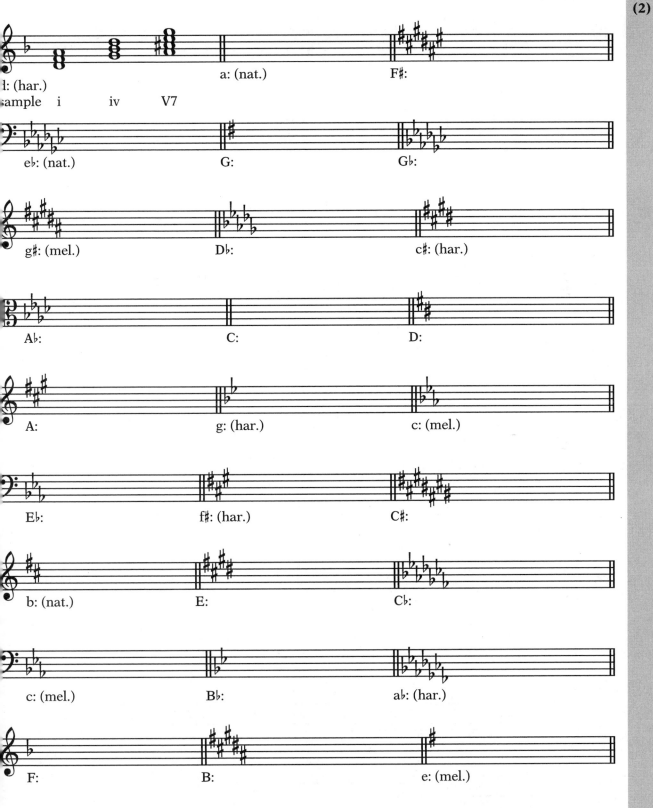

a: (nat.)   F#:

d: (har.)
sample   i   iv   V7

eb: (nat.)   G: Gb:

g#: (mel.)   Db: c#: (har.)

Ab: C: D:

A: g: (har.)   c: (mel.)

Eb: f#: (har.)   C#:

b: (nat.)   E: Cb:

c: (mel.)   Bb: ab: (har.)

F: B: e: (mel.)

6a   1. Construct the indicated triads *above* the following notes. Please note that a majority of diminished triads above *flat notes* will require double flats (♭♭). Augmented chords above *sharp notes* will require double sharps (×).

6a   2. Construct the indicated triads using the given note as the *root* of the triad.

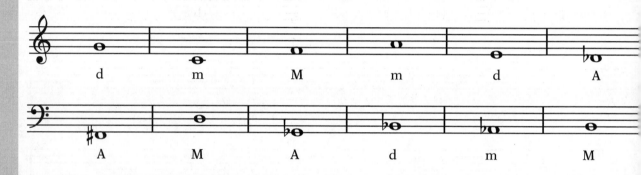

6a   3. Construct the indicated triads using the given note as the *third* of the triad.

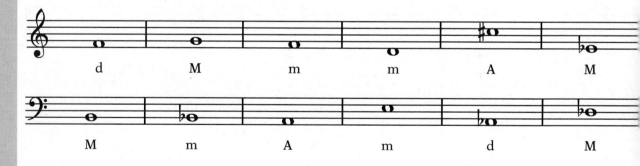

6a   4. Construct the indicated triads using the given note as the *fifth* of the triad.

Identify the following triads.

6c

Construct the following seventh chords using the given note as the *root* of the chord.

6f

Construct the following seventh chords using the given note as the *root* of the chord.

6f

Construct the following seventh chords using the given note as the *root* of the chord.

6f

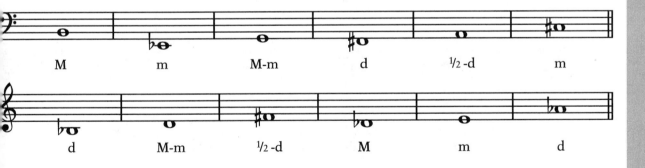

Construct seventh chords using the given note as the *third* of the chord.

6f

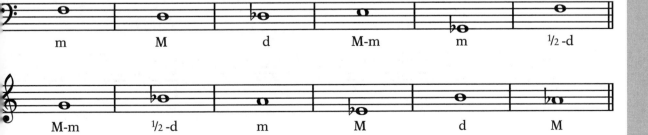

6f 9. Construct seventh chords using the given note as the *fifth* of the chord.

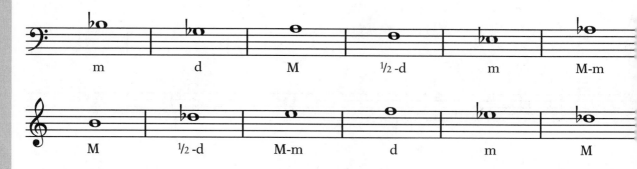

6f 10. Construct seventh chords using the given note as the *seventh* of the chord.

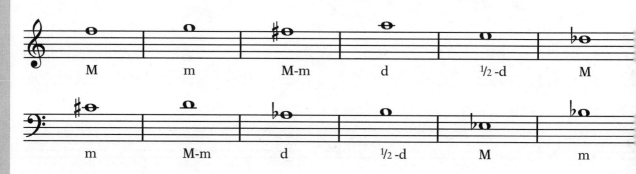

6f
(6)
(7) 11. Identify the following seventh chords.

6e
6f 12. Construct the primary chords—I-IV-V7 for major, i-iv-V7 for harmonic minor, and i-IV-V7 fo
(2)   (ascending) melodic minor—for the following major and minor keys.

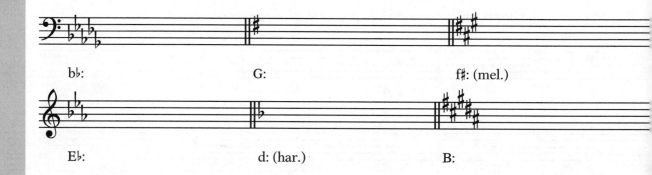

Unit 7

Rhythmic and Melodic Exercises—Difficult

7a MIXED RHYTHMIC UNITS

Any note may be subdivided into any number of notes. A quarter note, for example, regularly divide into two and subdivides into four, eight, and sixteen. But a quarter note may also be subdivided in three, five, six, seven, nine, etc. The desired number of notes is beamed or bracketed, with a numb placed above the beam or bracket to indicate the number of notes in the group.

In simple meters, the total durational value of the triplet (division into three) is always the same the value of the duplet (division into two). For example, the three eighths of a quarter-note triplet ha the same total value as the two eighths of the normal division. If the number of subdivided not exceeds twice the number in a regular division, the irregular group uses the next smaller note valu Thus, a quarter note subdivides into four, five, six, or seven sixteenth notes; for eight or more subdiv sions, into 32nd notes; and for sixteen or more subdivisions, into 64th notes.

The following examples show the same rhythmic pattern in three simple duple meters.

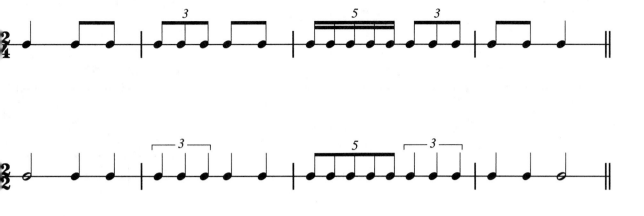

compound meters, the total durational value of the duplet (two) is always the same as the value of the triplet (the first division in compound meters). For example, the two eighths of a dotted-quarter-note triplet have the same value as the three eighths of the normal division. If the number of subdivided notes exceeds twice the number in a regular division, the same rule applies as in the simple duple meter. That is, a dotted quarter note subdivides into two, three, four, or five eighth notes; for six or more subdivisions, into sixteenth notes; and for twelve or more subdivisions, into 32nd notes.

etc.

he following examples show the same rhythmic pattern in three simple triple meters.

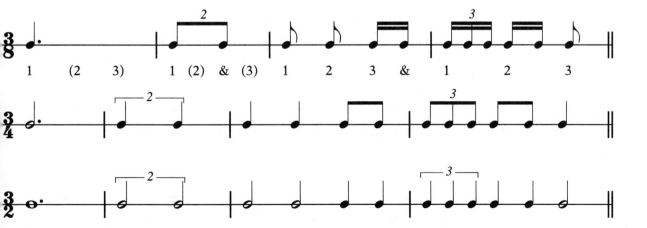

(1) SIMPLE AND COMPOUND METERS

2) EIGHT-MEASURE RHYTHMIC EXERCISES

Fine

D.C. al Fine

(3) COORDINATED-SKILL EXERCISES

7b MIXED METERS—CONSTANT NOTE VALUES

form of rhythmic and metric embellishment occurs when two different meter signatures are used in
he same work. Changing meter signatures during a work serves to shift the location of the strong beat.
1 the following examples of mixed meters, the *note value* of the beat remains constant.

(1) EIGHT-MEASURE RHYTHMIC EXERCISES

2) COORDINATED-SKILL EXERCISES

7c MIXED METERS—CHANGING NOTE VALUES

If simple and compound meter signatures are combined, the composer may indicate the relationship between note values above the staff. In the first example below, for instance, the notes above the staff indicate that the dotted quarter note in measure 2 equals the preceding quarter note, and that the quarter note in measure 3 equals the preceding dotted quarter note with the fundamental pulse or beat staying the same.

4) EIGHT-MEASURE RHYTHMIC EXERCISES

Fine

D.C. al Fine

(2) COORDINATED-SKILL EXERCISES

7d SYNCOPATION

yncopation is, generally speaking, a deliberate displacement of the normal pulse or beat of the meter.
ur sense of rhythm depends on the recurrence of groups of two or three equal beats each, with an
ccent on the first beat of each group. Any shifting of the accent to the normally weak beat(s) of the
easure is syncopation. The following examples show the same syncopated rhythmic pattern in three
mple duple meters.

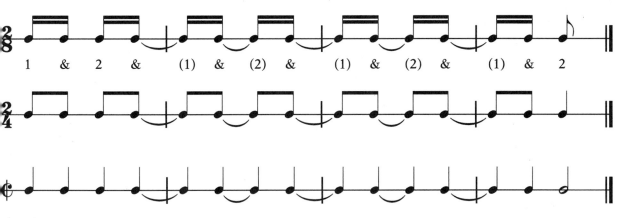

The following examples show the same syncopated rhythmic pattern in three simple triple meters.

1) EIGHT-MEASURE RHYTHMIC EXERCISES

Fine

D.C. al Fine

(2) COORDINATED-SKILL EXERCISES

3) THREE-PART RHYTHMIC EXERCISES

These exercises are for group participation, with at least one person on each line. Divide the parts among the performers, establish a beat, and begin. Perform each exercise a second and third time, with the performers tapping a different part each time.

A real test of your coordinated skills is to practice the exercises by yourself, tapping the bottom line with your foot, the middle line with your left hand, and the top line with your right hand.

See page 291.

Fine

D.C. al Fine

7e MELODIC EXERCISES

(1) MIXED RHYTHMIC UNITS

(2) COORDINATED MELODIC-RHYTHMIC EXERCISES

) MIXED METERS—CONSTANT NOTE VALUES

(4) COORDINATED MELODIC-RHYTHMIC EXERCISES

Fine

D.C. al Fine

5) MIXED METERS—CHANGING NOTE VALUES

Fine

D.C. al Fine

(6) COORDINATED MELODIC-RHYTHMIC EXERCISES

Fine

D.C. al Fine

7) SYNCOPATION

(fi)

246

8) COORDINATED MELODIC-RHYTHMIC EXERCISES

(9) CHURCH MODES AND OTHER SCALE FORMS

The solfeggio system (see 5b) can also be used for sight singing music in the church modes (see 3o). examples 1–5 below, the syllables indicated are for the movable-*do* system. In singing such example the fixed-*do* system may be used as well, or use *la* as a substitute for solfeggio or letter names.

Melodic Writing and Transposition

8a MELODIC WRITING

Writing melodies is a goal of most beginning students of music theory. Composing the "great" melody is as much luck as it is a skill, but some very general rules may help you begin this rather personal and complex task. Remember that some of the most memorable melodies are the simplest and most direct in form.

Melodic lines are divided into "periods," comparable to a sentence of written prose. A completed melody will be made up of several periods, usually of even numbers, 2, 4 or 8.
A "period" will be four, eight, or possibly 16 measures in length.
Each "period" has two or sometimes more "phrases." Phrases are usually structured in a question (antecedent)—answer (consequent) format. The first phrase (antecedent) ends on a pitch other than the tonic (see 6b) and the second phrase (consequent) ends on the tonic.

← ———— antecedent ———— → | ← ———— consequent ———— → |

A period may be parallel in form (first and second phrases are similar) or contrasting in form (first and second phrases are not similar).

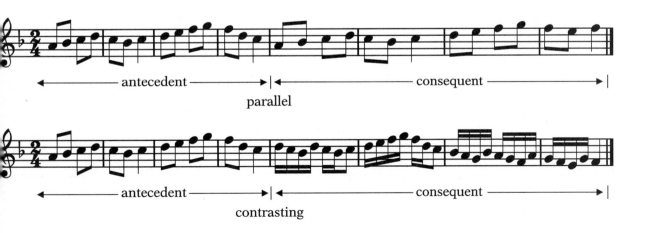

← ———— antecedent ———— → | ← ———— consequent ———— → |
parallel

← ———— antecedent ———— → | ← ———— consequent ———— → |
contrasting

5. Melodic lines have an overall "architecture." A few possible shapes are: an undulating line, an arching line, a falling line, and a rising line. Differing shapes can be combined and the possibilities of differing shapes and combinations are extensive.

Undulating Line:

Arching Line:

Falling Line:

Rising Line:

A melody is made up of two compnoents—pitch and rhythm. Many times the strength of a melody lies in a repeated rhythmic pattern, or a unique pattern of pitches or intervals, but most often, a combination of both.

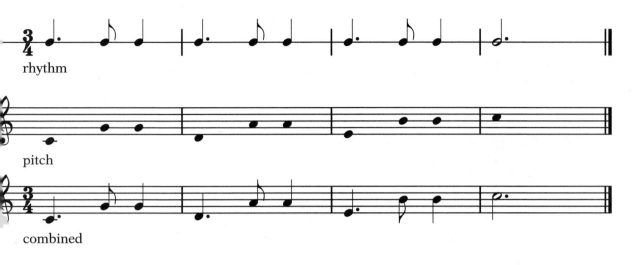

Melodic lines may move by (a) scale steps with few interval skips (conjunct motion), (b) outlined chords, or (c) wide interval leaps (disjunct motion—more common in instrumental music than in vocal), or in combination. The overall range (lowest to highest note) of a melody will be dictated by the instrument or voice for which you are writing. The vocal range (tessitura) of the untrained voice is at maximum approximately an octave and a fifth.

8. Ascending musical lines generate more energy and drama, descending musical lines less energy an
a sense of repose.

←——————— tension ———————→ | ←——— relaxation ———→

8b TRANSPOSITION

To **transpose** a melody or composition is to rewrite or perform it in a different key than the origin
Transposition is an essential skill for singers who wish to perform a piece in a more comfortable ran
and it is a skill required for accompanists, conductors, composers, and some instrumentalists.

(1) SHIFTING NOTES ON THE STAFF

There are three methods of transposition. The first, and most common, is the shifting of notes on t
staff to the new key. For example, if you wanted to transpose a melody from C to E♭ major (up a min
third), you would write every note *up* a minor third and add the new key signature (three flats), as
the example below. Note that you could also write every note *down* a major sixth, in accordance wi
the principles of interval inversion (see 4f3).

Melody to Be Transposed

original key: C

to E♭: up a minor third

to E♭: down a major sixth

It is easy to check your work in this method of transposition by remembering that the movable-
solfeggio syllables and the scale-degree numbers of the transposed melody will always be the sar
as those of the original key. In the example above, the melody begins do-re-mi-re-mi-fa-sol-
(1-2-3-2-3-4-5-4) in both C and E♭, and in whatever other key you transpose the melody to—*if* you ha
moved the notes correctly.

2) TRANSPOSITION BY SCALE DEGREES

A second method of transposition is through the use of scale degrees; exchanging the appropriate scale degree of the original key with the scale degree of the new one.

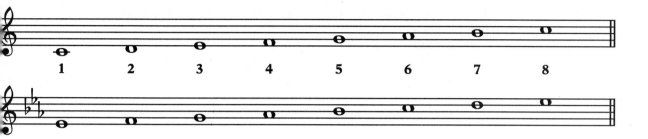

For example, in the melody below, the first scale degree (tonic) of the original key is exchanged for the first scale degree of the new one, the fifth scale degree (dominant) of the original key is exchanged for the fifth scale degree of the new one, and so on.

3) CHANGING THE CLEF

A third method of transposition is to change the *clef* instead of the notes on the staff. In this method, to change a melody, you would simply alter the clef sign and add the new key signature. This method, which is used in some conservatories, has the advantage of not requiring the complete rewriting of a melody or piece, but you must be familiar with all seven clefs (see 1b).

(4) INSTRUMENTAL TRANSPOSITION

There are a number of orchestral instruments that *transpose*. These instruments, for historical an acoustical reasons, were written in keys other than that of their actual sound. The clarinet, French hor trumpet, and saxophone are transposing instruments. Their *given* key, based on their individual over tone series (see 3c), is the pitch they play if they play the note C. The B♭ clarinet is a B♭ instrument. If th B♭ clarinet plays C it will sound B♭, a major 2nd *lower*. Therefore, if you write for the B♭ clarinet yo must transpose *up* a major 2nd. If the F French horn plays C it will sound F, a perfect 5th *lower*. Ther fore, if you write for the F French horn you must transpose *up* a perfect 5th.

Instruments that sound their actual pitch are nontransposing, *concert-pitched*, or C instrument The violin, viola, cello, flute, oboe, bassoon, trombone, and tuba are nontransposing. The piccolo an string bass are also C instruments. The piccolo sounds one octave higher than written and the strir bass sounds one octave lower than written.

Following is a list of the transposing instruments. For each, the note C is given and the *actual soun* *ing pitch* is also given.

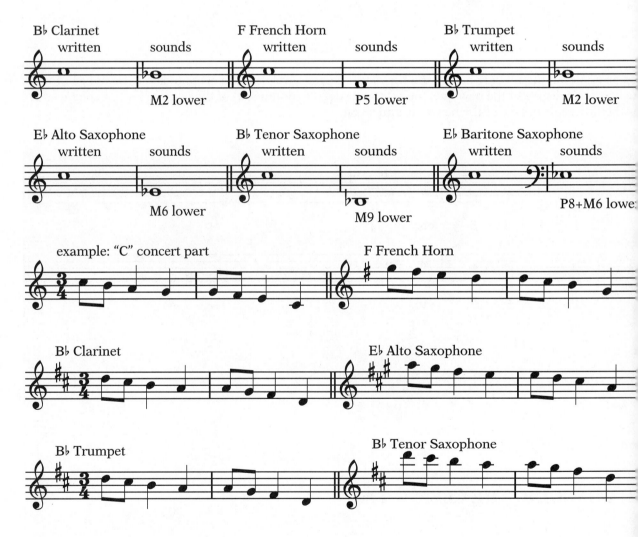

Please note that the baritone saxophone is a bass instrument but is written in the treble clef. Th saxophones are all written in treble clef to allow the performer to play all of the instruments withou the need of clef changes.

254

In this excerpt from *Götterdämmerung (Twilight of the Gods)* by Richard Wagner (1813–1883), French horns and trumpets vary transpositions throughout the work. The different transpositions are indicated separately throughout the score. The tenor (B♭) and bass (F) tubas sound an octave lower *plus* the B♭ and transpositions. (All transpositions are below the given note.) The string bass sounds an octave lower than written.

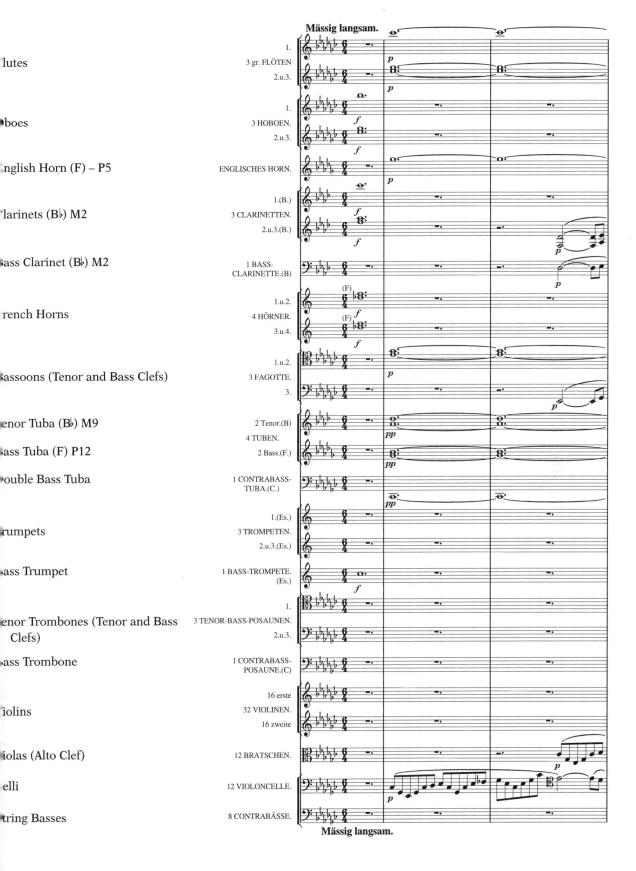

8a

1. Complete the following periods in *parallel* form.

2. Complete the following periods in *contrasting* form.

3. Write an opening phrase for the following periods in *parallel* form.

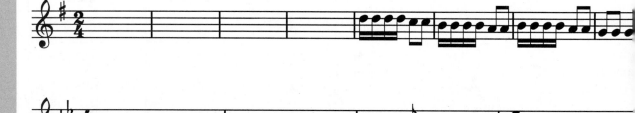

4. Write an opening phrase for the following periods in *contrasting* form.

8a

8a   1. Write a period with an opening phrase and a closing phrase in an undulating line.

b min:

2. Write a period with an opening phrase and a closing phrase in an arching line.

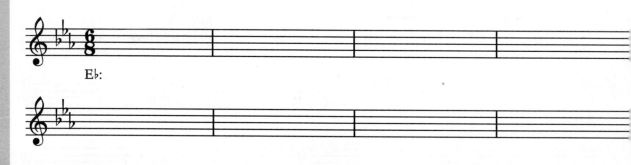

Eb:

3. Write a period with an opening phrase and a closing phrase in a "falling line" shape.

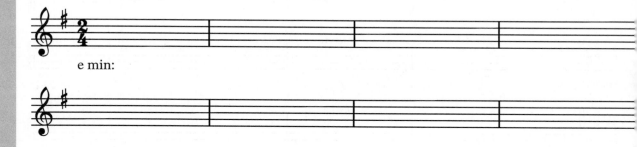

e min:

4. Write a period with an opening phrase and a closing phrase in a "rising line" shape.

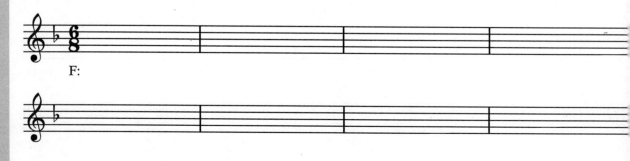

F:

In the following exercises, establish the new key signature and transpose the notes up or down as indicated.

1. Transpose up from C to E.

2. Transpose down from C to F.

3. Transpose up from C to A♭.

4. Transpose down from C to D.

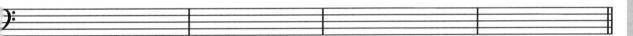

5. Transpose up from C to G.

6. Transpose down from C to B♭.

7. Transpose up from C to A.

8. Transpose down from C to E♭.

8b
(1)
(2)
In the following exercise, establish the new key signature and transpose the notes up or down indicated.

1. Transpose up from B♭ to E.

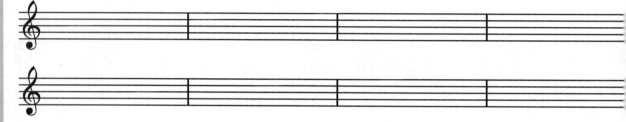

2. Transpose down from B♭ to F.

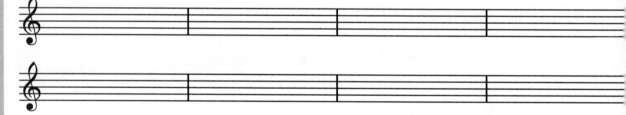

3. Transpose up from B♭ to C.

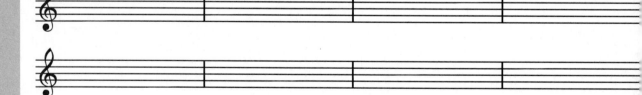

4. Transpose down from B♭ to D.

NAME _____

In the following exercise, establish the new key signature and transpose the notes up or down as indicated.

1. Transpose up from F to G.

2. Transpose down from F to B♭.

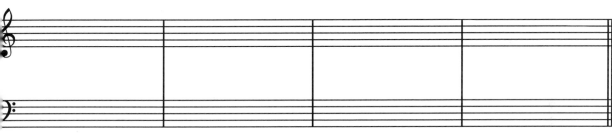

3. Transpose up from F to A.

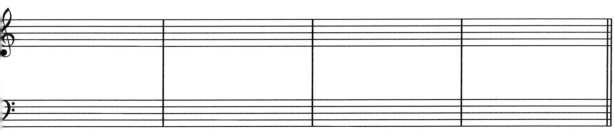

4. Transpose down from F to E♭.

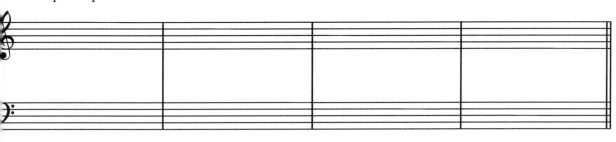

8b
(4)

In the following instrumental transpositions, establish the new key and transpose the notes as require

B♭ Clarinet

B♭ Trumpet

E♭ Baritone Saxophone

F French Horn

B♭ Tenor Saxophone

. In the following exercises, establish the new key signature and transpose the notes up or down as indicated.

Transpose up from G to B♭.

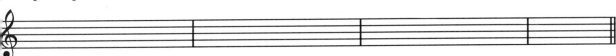

Transpose down from g mi to a mi.

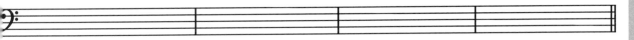

. In the following instrumental transpositions, establish the new key and transpose the notes as required.

E♭ Alto Saxophone

B♭ Trumpet

Unit 9

Chord Progressions and Harmonization

9a DOUBLING TRIADS AND SEVENTH CHORDS

Traditional harmony is usually framed in four parts: bass, tenor, alto, and soprano; therefore, doubling a note in a triad will be necessary. There are good reasons why certain doublings in both traditional and commercial music are preferable. The following generally apply to triads:

- A triad in root position doubles the root. In the root position it is not unusual to triple the root and exclude the fifth. This tripling of the root is allowable because the second overtone (3c), the perfect fifth above the root, is so powerful that its presence is easily heard.
- A triad in its first inversion doubles the soprano note.
- A triad in its second inversion doubles the fifth.
- In seventh chords there is no need for doubling; however, the fifth of the root position seventh chord may be excluded and the root doubled for the same reason that the root may be tripled in the root-position triad.
- Avoid doubling the leading tone (3a) and the seventh of any seventh chord.
- In traditional four-part writing, spacing—distance between notes—is generally greater between the lower two notes and closer in the upper notes. Intervals larger than an octave are common between the two lowest notes, but should be avoided between the tenor and alto, alto and soprano.

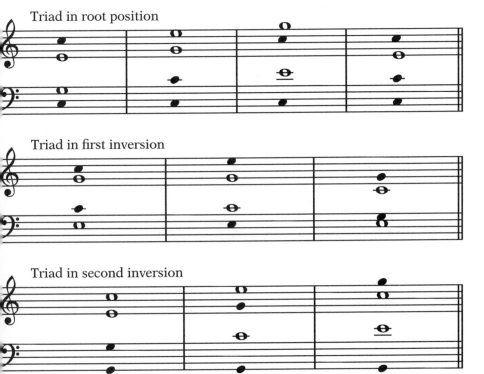

Triad in root position

Triad in first inversion

Triad in second inversion

Chord spacing

weak   strong   weak   strong

9b CHORD PROGRESSIONS

Moving from one chord to another, a progression, is best accomplished with but a few basic rules. These rules represent traditional practices, but one may find many exceptions in music literature.

(1) COMMON TONES

When common tones are found between adjoining chords, it is best to maintain them from one chord to the other.

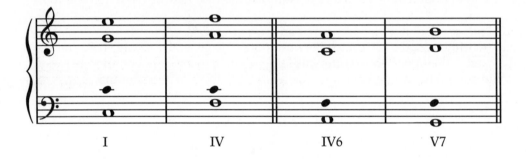

    I   IV   IV6   V7

(2) HORIZONTAL LINE MOVEMENT

For a better melodic line, it is preferable to move voices smoothly, avoiding large intervallic leaps. However, the lowest voice may frequently move by larger intervals. Outer voices should move in contrary motion.

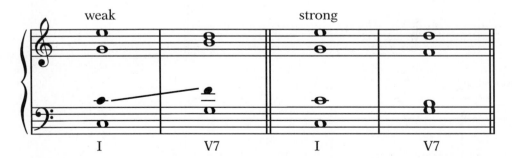

    I   V7   I   V7

3) PARALLEL MOVEMENT

Avoid parallel fifths and parallel octaves.

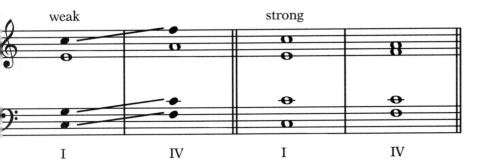

4) THE CADENCE

A cadence is the last two chords found at the end of (2) phrase(s) or a period (8a). The three most common cadences are the *authentic* cadence, *half* cadence, and *plagal* cadence.

Authentic cadence

The last two chords of a work. The chords in *root* position are dominant to tonic.

The authentic cadence is *perfect* if the tonic tone, in the final tonic chord, is in the soprano (top voice). The cadence is *imperfect* if, in the final tonic chord, the soprano note is the third or fifth of the chord.

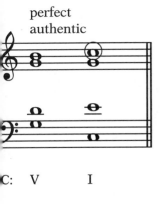
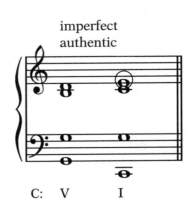
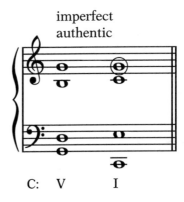

Half Cadence

A half cadence ends on any chord other than the tonic. This cadence is frequently found at the end o the first phrase of a period or the end of a first ending (1m2), and most commonly is tonic to dominan

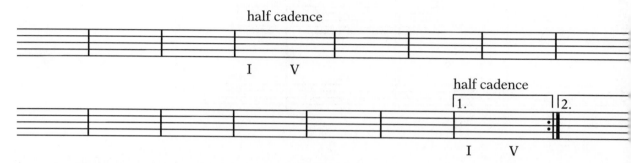

The dominant chord is an *active* chord demanding an answer or forward motion. Placing the dominan at the end of the first phrase or first ending creates a feeling of a continuation of the musical line (i.e like a comma in a sentence). Half cadences are not perfect or imperfect.

Plagal Cadence

In the plagal cadence the chord progression is from subdominant to tonic. This is not a frequently see cadence but is added to the end of a hymn—the *"amen"* cadence.

Similar to the authenic cadence, the plagal cadence is *perfect* if the tonic tone in the final chord is in th soprano. The cadence is *imperfect* if in the final tonic chord the soprano note is the third or fifth of th chord.

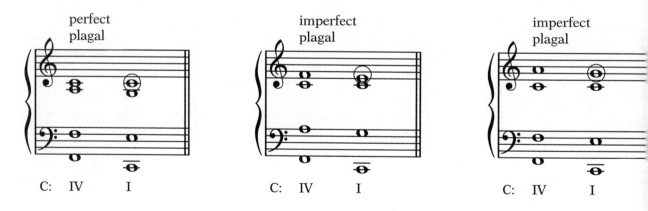

9c HARMONIZATION

Adding an accompaniment, or musical background, to a melody is called **harmonization.** Most melodies can be harmonized simply, using only the primary triads I, IV, and V (see 6c). Being able to improvise an accompaniment to a song or folk tune is fun, and you need not be an expert pianist to learn to do it. The following guidelines are very general, but they will help you to establish the key of a melody and to decide which chord or chords you will use in each measure.

. Establish the key of the melody in any or all of the following three ways:
   a. Look at the key signature.
   b. Look at the first and the last tones of the melody.
   c. See if the implied chords at the beginning of the first full measure and at the end of the last measure are the same. Generally they are, and this chord is the tonic (I).
. Once you have verified the key, establish the primary chords (I, IV, V, or V7) in that key.
. The accompaniment chords should contain the tones found in the melody. Tones on strong beats are more important than tones on weaker beats (see 1g).
. Some tones in the melody may not belong to the accompaniment chords. These are nonharmonic tones, which are discussed in the following section.

1) NONHARMONIC TONES

Nonharmonic tones are any tones in a melody that are not included in the underlying chord (or harmony). There are many kinds of nonharmonic tones. Seven of the most important are discussed here.

(a) Passing Tones

Passing tones occur stepwise between two chord tones. In the examples below, the passing tones are circled. In each case, they "pass" from one tone of the C major triad to another tone of the triad. All the passing tones in these examples are *unaccented* passing tones, since they occur on the weak part of the beat.

Accented passing tones occur on the strong part of the beat, as in the following examples.

Neighboring Tones

Neighboring tones, or auxiliary tones, occur stepwise above or below a repeated chord tone. A neighboring tone may be diatonic or chromatic, unaccented or accented. In the following examples, (a) shows upper neighboring tones and (b) shows lower neighboring tones. All are unaccented.

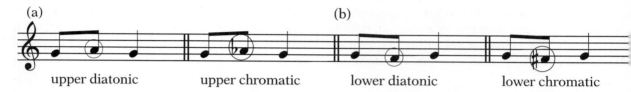

| upper diatonic | upper chromatic | lower diatonic | lower chromatic |

In examples (c) and (d) below, the neighboring tones are accented, occuring on the strong part of the beat.

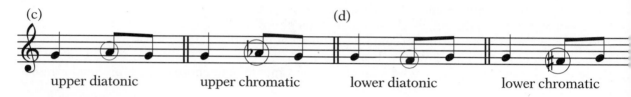

| upper diatonic | upper chromatic | lower diatonic | lower chromatic |

Escape Tones

An *escape tone* is a nonharmonic note approached by *step* that resolved by *leap;* the resolution is usual in the opposite direction.

Appoggiatura

An *appoggiatura* is a note approached by a *leap* and resolved by a *step,* usually in the opposite direction

Anticipation

An *anticipation* is a nonharmonic note that anticipates a harmonic note of the following chord.

Suspension—Retardation

A *suspension* is a harmonic note that has been suspended into the following chord and is resolve stepwise down. A *retardation* is similar but resolves stepwise up.

suspension   retardation

270

Pedal Point

A *pedal point* is a note, generally in the bass, that is sustained while other parts have changing harmonies.

Pedal Point   Inverted Pedal

(2) ADDING AN ACCOMPANIMENT

An accompaniment consisting only of root-position primary chords is dull to listen to and awkward to play. For these reasons, the most common accompaniment progression is root-position tonic, second-inversion subdominant, and first-inversion dominant seventh. For further ease in performance, the *fifth* of the dominant seventh is usually omitted. This progression is shown below in all major keys, in circle-of-fifths order. (The starred progressions are enharmonic equivalents.) Although the progression is generally played with the left hand, it can readily be played with the right hand if the melody is in the bass. Left-hand fingerings are included in the first example, and the same fingerings should be used in every key.

Practice this pattern until you are comfortable with it in all major keys. You should also practice it throughout the *minor* circle of fifths.

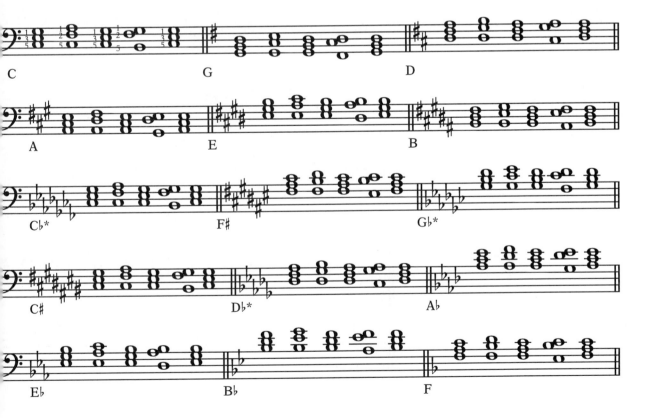

The following two-hand progression is useful in accompanying an instrumental or vocal soloist group. This progression is shown in all major keys, in circle-of-fifths order. (The starred progressions are enharmonic equivalents.) Practice until you are comfortable in all major keys; then also practice throughout the *minor* circle of fifths.

3) ACCOMPANIMENT PATTERNS

The following patterns are just a sampling of the almost endless possibilities for varying the primary chords. Experiment and devise other patterns; also try using more than one pattern in a single accompaniment. The patterns are written in simple meters, but they are easily adaptable to compound meters.

Patterns in $\frac{2}{4}$

(Alberti bass)

Patterns in $\frac{3}{4}$

Patterns in 4/4

(Alberti bass)

Pop Patterns

"blue note"

(Boogie-woogie)

(1950s Rock and Roll)

275

9d FIGURED BASS

Figured bass (or thorough bass) is a numerical method of indicating the chords to be played above a given bass line. In the Baroque period (roughly 1600–1750), keyboard players improvised their part from these figures—that is, their part was not written out in their score; it consisted only of the bass line of the composition with figures for the chords beneath it. These figured-bass symbols are still extensively used in the early stages of the study of music theory.

The figures are simple indications of the *intervals above the bass tone* of a chord. Not every interval is indicated in the figured bass, which is abbreviated for ease of reading. For example, a bass tone without any figures indicates a triad in root position, and the other figures that are in parentheses in the examples below are also generally omitted. Chromatic alterations are indicated by the symbols shown.

(1) FIGURED-BASS SYMBOLS FOR TRIADS

   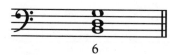   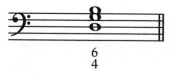

(5) root-position triad;
(3) the bass tone is the root of the triad

6 first inversion of the triad;
(3) the bass tone is the third of the triad

6 second inversion of a triad;
4 the bass tone is the fifth of the triad

(2) REALIZATION

Translating the Arabic numbers into the correct notes above the given bass line is simple, but in performance practice can be very difficult. In "realization," the performer uses the figured bass only as an outline for a more complex "improvised" accompaniment that complements the overall musical work.

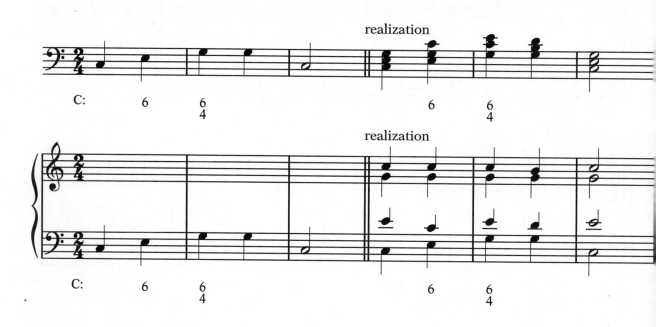

276

3) FIGURED-BASS SYMBOLS FOR SEVENTH CHORDS

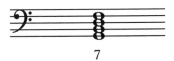

7

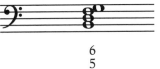

6
5

7
5) root-position seventh chord; the bass tone is
3) the root of the chord

6   first inversion of a seventh chord; the bass
5   tone is the third of the chord
(3)

4
3

4
2

6)
4   second inversion of a seventh chord; the
3   bass tone is the fifth of the chord

(6) third inversion of a seventh chord; the bass
4   tone is the seventh of the chord
2

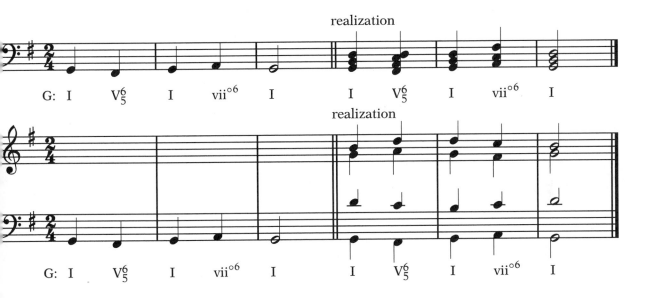

277

(4) CHROMATIC ALTERATIONS

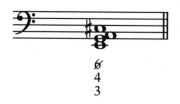

the chord is
◦ diminished or
⁺ augmented

a diagonal line through
a number raises the tone
one half step

♯ when used *alone,* these accidentals affect the
♭ *third* of a root-position chord
♮

♯ when *preceding a number,* these accidentals
♭ indicate a corresponding alteration of the tone
♮ represented by that number

(5) INVERSIONS

In the study of music theory, the figured bass is used to indicate if a chord is root position or an inversion. In commercial music, letters are placed above the staff to indicate the desired chord. Inversions of the chord are indicated by first the chord letter, a slash mark, and then the desired *root note* (bass note) placed below. C over E would be a first invesion, C over G a second inversion.

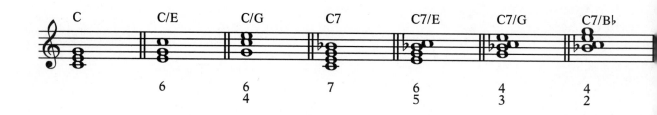

In the following examples, circle and label the nonharmonic tones.

UPT	unaccented passing tone	E	escape tone
APT	accented passing tone	App	appoggiatura
UN	upper neighboring (auxiliary) tone	A	anticipation
LN	lower neighboring (auxiliary) tone	S	suspension
		R	retardation

9C
(1)
(2)

In the following melodies, establish the correct primary chords, circle and label the nonharmonic tone and then write two possible accompaniment patterns.

1.

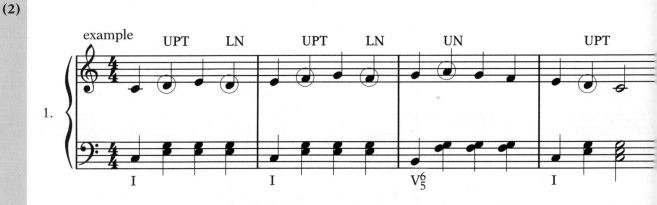

2.

9C
(1)
(2)

9d

(1)   Construct appropriate chords above the following figured-bass symbols. Label the chords to indica their root-position name and quality.

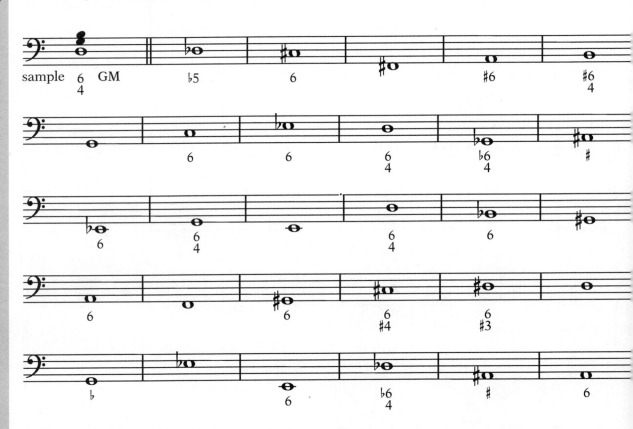

9d

(1)   Note the key in each of the following exercises, then label the chords by Roman numerals and a Arabic numbers to indicate the inversion.

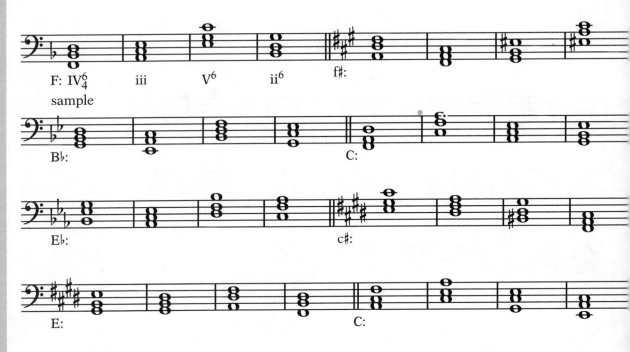

NAME _____

Construct appropriate chords above the following figured-bass symbols. Label the chords to indicate their root-position name and quality.

Note the key in each of the following exercises, then label the chords by Roman numerals and add Arabic numbers to indicate the inversion.

9c
(1)

1. In the following examples circle and label nonharmonic tones.

2. In the following melodies, establish the correct primary chords, circle and label the nonharmonic tones, and write an accompaniment.

9c
(1)
(2)

3. Note the key given, then label the chords by Roman numerals and Arabic numbers to indicate the inversion.

9d
(1)
(3)
(4)

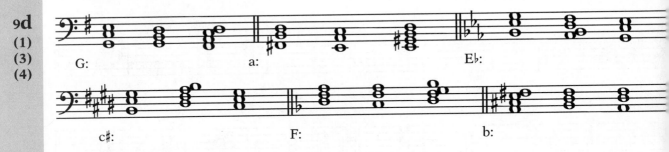

4. Construct appropriate chords above the following figured-bass symbols. Label the chords and indicate their root-position name and quality.

9d
(1)
(3)
(4)

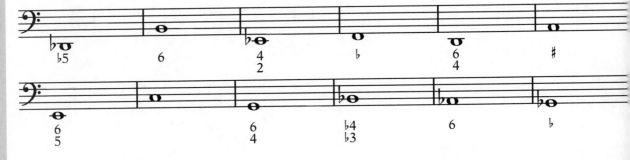

APPENDIX: Terms, Signs, and Symbols

he following lists are necessarily not comprehensive. You should consult the Contents for terms and oncepts defined and discussed in the text, and one of the standard music dictionaries for other terms, struments, and symbols not included here.

10a GENERAL MUSIC TERMS

cappella (It., "in chapel style") for unaccompanied voices

cidental a sharp, flat, or natural introduced within a work—in contrast to the sharps or flats found in the key signature

berti bass a keyboard accompaniment played by the left hand, in which chord tones alternate in a fixed pattern

la breve (cut time, ¢) simple duple meter with the half note as the beat

acrusis upbeat or pick-up

ia song from opera or oratorio with instrumental accompaniment

peggio see Signs and Symbols (10e)

ymmetric meter a meter such as $\frac{5}{8}$ or $\frac{7}{4}$, with unequal division of the measure so that accents occur irregularly

onal without tonality; not in a key

igmentation increasing, usually doubling, the length of a note or passage

thentic cadence the harmonic progression V7-I used at the end of a phrase or composition

sso continuo same as figured bass (see 9d)

am a horizontal line, in place of flags, for groups of notes shorter than quarter notes

dence a point of repose at the end of a phrase, section, or composition

denza a solo passage in improvisatory style

ord a group of notes sounding simultaneously

romatic any nondiatonic tone introduced into a scale

romatic scale a scale including all twelve tones within an octave

vier any keyboard instrument

clef a sign written at the beginning of the staff to indicate the pitch name for a given line

coda a strongly conclusive final section of a movement or composition; *codetta*: a small coda

common time (**c**) $\frac{4}{4}$ time

compound interval an interval greater than an octave

consonance a stable combination of tones that does not require resolution

contrapuntal pertaining to counterpoint

counterpoint music consisting of two or more independent lines

cut time see *alla breve*

deceptive cadence the harmonic progression V-VI (instead of V-I) at the end of a phrase

diatonic a term describing the notes of the major or natural minor scale, excluding all chromatic alterations

diminution decreasing, usually halving, the length of a note or passage

dissonance an unstable combination of tones that requires resolution

doppio double

downbeat the first beat of a measure

duplet a group of two notes in compound meter equal to three of the same notes

enharmonic equivalents tones that are named differently but sound the same

equal temperament a system of tuning in which the octave is divided into twelve equal intervals

figured bass numerical indication of intervals above a bass tone

flag or *hook* a small flag added to a stem for notes shorter than a quarter note *grace note* see Signs and Symbols (10e)

Great Staff a double staff with both a treble clef and a bass clef

ground bass a phrase continuously repeated in the bass

half cadence an incomplete cadence, usually on dominant harmony

homophony music in which a melody, usually in the highest voice, is supported by a chordal accompaniment

interval distance between two notes

intonation accuracy of pitch in singing or playing tones

key signature one or more sharps or flats grouped at the beginning of the staff indicating what notes are to be altered throughout the piece

ledger line a small line for notes added above or below the staff

maggiore major

meter signature the two numbers at the beginning of a piece indicating a recurring pattern of accented and unaccented beats. The top number indicates the number of beats grouped into each measure; the bottom number indicates the note value of the beat

metronome a pendulum or electronic device used to determine and regulate tempo

minore minor

mode any scale form; before about 1600, usually one of the church modes; after about 1600, usually major or minor

modulation change of key in the course of a composition

monophony music consisting of a single unaccompanied melody

opus (op.) a musical composition (usually accompanied by a number); the works of a composer are numbered consecutively—op. 1, op. 2, etc.—in order of composition or publication

ostinato (It., "obstinate") a figure or phrase continuously repeated throughout a passage or composition

ottava (8, 8va) octave

pentatonic five-pitch scale—in contrast to the seven-pitch major and minor scales

pianoforte the original, unabbreviated name for the piano

pitch a musical sound as measured by how low or high it is within a scale

plagal cadence the harmonic progression IV-I (th "amen" cadence)

polychord a combination of two or more differen chords

polyphony see *counterpoint*

polytonality the simultaneous use of two or mor tonal centers or keys

primary triads triads above the first, fourth, an fifth pitches of a major or minor scale

prime perfect unison

resolution the progression of a dissonant interva or chord to a consonant (stable) interval o chord

root the lowest note of a chord

scale an ordered series of pitches going either u or down

scherzo (It., "joke") a brusque or humorous com position in triple meter; a scherzo is some times used in symphonies, sonatas, etc., i place of a minuet

segno sign

sequence the immediate duplication of a tona pattern in the same part(s) at a different pitch

simple interval an interval of an octave or less

slur a curved line connecting two or more note of different pitch. Indicates that the notes ar to be played smoothly connected

staff a series of five lines and four spaces o which notes are written

stem a vertical line added to the note head on a notes except the whole note

tempo the rate of speed of a musical compositio

thorough bass same as figured bass (see 9d)

tie a curved line connecting two notes of th same pitch

timbre tone color or quality

tone row same as twelve-tone row (see 3q)

tonic the name and beginning pitch of a major minor scale

transposition performance in a key other than th original

triad a three-note chord combining a root and th intervals of a third and a fifth above the root

triplet a group of three notes in simple met equal to two of the same notes

tritone an interval of three whole steps—A4 or d

10b PERFORMANCE TERMS

ccelerando (accel.) increasing in tempo

dagio leisurely, slow; *adagietto*: a little faster than adagio

d libitum (ad lib.) at will; at the performer's discretion

ffrettando (affrett.) hurrying

gitato in an agitated or excited manner

l fine (repeat) to the end

llargando (allarg.) decreasing in tempo

llegro fast; *allegretto*: slightly slower than allegro

ll'ottava (8va----¬) when above the notes: play an octave higher; when below the notes: play an octave lower

ndante moderately slow: *andantino*: slightly faster than andante

nimato with animation

piacere at pleasure; without measured tempo

ppassionata passionately

rco bow; with the bow

ssai very

tempo return to the first tempo

ttacca proceed to the next section or movement without pause

rio fire; vigor

lando (cal.) decreasing in tempo and loudness

ntabile (cantab.), *cantando, cantante* in singing style

n with

escendo (cresc.) increasing in loudness

capo (D.C.) (repeat) from the beginning

l segno (D.S.) (repeat) from the sign

crescendo (decresc.) decreasing in loudness

minuendo (dim., dimin.) decreasing in loudness

visi (div.) divided; an indication that a vocal or instrumental section is to divide and perform two or more parts

lce (dol.) sweetly

loroso sadly; plaintively

ergico with energy

pressivo (espr., espress.) expressively

mata see Signs and Symbols (10e)

e the end; the concluding point after a return to the beginning or to a sign

rte (*f*) loud; *fortissimo* (*ff*): very loud

rte-piano (*fp*) loud, then immediately soft

rza fire; forcefulness

coso playfully

sto strict; exact

ssando a sliding-pitch effect

P. (grand pause) silence; a rest for the entire orchestra or ensemble

ve slow; solemnly, seriously

zioso gracefully

hold same as fermata (see Signs and Symbols, 10e)

largo broad; very slow; *larghetto*: slightly faster than largo; *larghissimo*: the slowest tempo indication

legato (leg.) very smooth, with no separation between notes (see Signs and Symbols, 10e)

lento slow, but not as slow as largo

l'istesso tempo the same tempo

loco as written (used after *all'ottava*)

maestoso majestically

marcato (marc.) marked; stressed

marziale martially

meno mosso, meno moto with less movement; slower

mezzo half; moderately

mezzo forte (*mf*) not as loud as forte; *mezzo piano* (*mp*): not as soft as piano

misterioso mysteriously

M.M. (Maelzel metronome) used with a number to indicate tempo; the number indicates beats per minute

moderato moderate (tempo)

molto very

morendo (mor.) dying away; fading

mosso, moto motion

non not

ossia otherwise; indicates another way of performing a passage

pesante (pes.) heavily

piano (*p*) soft; *pianissimo* (*pp*): very soft

più more

più mosso, più moto with more movement; faster

pizzicato (pizz.) plucked (instead of bowed, in string parts)

poco little; a little

presto very fast; *prestissimo*: faster than presto; the fastest tempo indication

quasi in the manner of

rallentando (rall.) gradually slowing

rinforzando (rf., rfz., rinf.) reinforced; suddenly stressed

ritardando (rit., ritard.) gradually slowing

ritenuto holding back; immediately slower

rubato with rhythmic freedom

scherzando playfully

secco dry; drily

segue follows; continues in the same way

sempre (sem., semp.) always; throughout

senza without

sforzando (*sf*, *sfz*) with force; with an explosive accent

simile similarly; in the same way

sordino mute

sostenuto (sost.) sustained

sotto under; below

staccato (stacc.) detached; separated (see Signs and Symbols, 10e)

stringendo (string.) accelerating markedly; hastening

subito suddenly

tacet silent; a part so marked is silent for the entire section or movement

tanto much; so much

tempo I, tempo primo return to the first tempo

tenuto (ten.) held; sustained for full value

tremolo ("trembling") the rapid repetition of one note or the rapid alternation of two notes

troppo too much

una corda (u.c.) a piano indication of the use of the soft pedal

vibrato (vib.) slight fluctuation of pitch or intensity

vivace spirited, lively; vivacissimo: very spirited, very lively

vivo lively

(1) A SCALE OF SPEEDS (TEMPOS)

	Largo		Lento			Andantino		Allegretto				Prestissimo
Larghissimo		Grave		Adagio		Andante	Moderato		Allegro	Vivace	Presto	

SLOWER ← ————————————————————————————— → FASTER

(2) TERMS REFERRING TO TEMPO

larghissimo very slow

largo slow

grave slow and solemn

lento slow, but not dragging

adagio slow, leisurely, a slow rate of movement

andante a moderately slow rate of movement, with the feeling of moving along or flowing

andantino moderately slow, but with a little more motion than andante (diminutive of andante)

moderato moderately, in moderate tempo

allegretto moderately fast (diminutive of allegro)

allegro rapid, lively, a brisk rate of movement

vivace fast, vivaciously

presto very fast, quickly, rapidly

prestissimo very quickly, as fast as possible

(3) TERMS REFERRING TO VARIATIONS IN TEMPO

a tempo in time, return to the previous tempo after a deviation or relaxation

tempo primo (tempo I^{mo}) return to the original tempo of the piece

accelerando (accel.) a gradual quickening of tempo

stringendo (string.) hastening, accelerating the movement, usually suddenly and rapidly with a crescendo

ritardando (rit. or ritard.) a gradual slowing tempo

ritenuto a holding back of the tempo, but without a continuous slowing down

allargando (allarg.) gradually slower and louder with a sense of increasing power

morendo gradually slower and softer, dying away

10c Instruments of the Orchestra

glish Name	Italian Name	French Name	German Name
ıte	Flauto	Flûte	Flöte
›oe	Oboe	Hautbois	Oboe (or Hoboe)
arinet	Clarinetto	Clarinette	Klarinette
ssoon	Fagotto	Basson	Fagott
›rn	Corno	Cor	Horn
ımpet	Tromba	Trompette	Trompete
›mbone	Trombone	Trombone	Posaune
ba	Tuba	Tuba	Tuba (or Bass tuba)
npani (or kettledrums)	Timpani	Timbales	Pauken
ırp	Arpa	Harpe	Harfe
›lin	Violino	Violon	Geige (or Violine)
›la	Viola	Alto	Bratsche (or Viole)
›loncello (or cello)	Violoncello	Violoncelle	Violoncello
uble Bass (or contrabass)	Contrabasso	Contrebasse	Kontrabass

10d Voice Types

prano high female voice
•zzo-soprano medium female voice
•o low female voice
•ntralto lowest female voice

Tenor high male voice
Baritone medium male voice
Bass low male voice

10e Signs and Symbols

cent	> or –	either mark, placed above or below a note, indicates that emphasis should be added to the affected note.

›ato slur	a curved line placed over or under several different notes. The slur indicates that the notes should be played very smoothly. Legato is the opposite of staccato (see below).

›ccato dot	•	a dot placed above or below a note. Staccato dots indicate that the affected note should be shortened and detached from the other notes.

appoggiatura		a nonharmonic, ornamental tone that precedes a chord tone. Unlike the grace note (see below), the appoggiatura is subject to a strict beat.

sounds

grace note		a nonharmonic, ornamental tone that precedes a chord tone. The grace note is not subject to a strict beat.

sounds

breath mark	**,**	indicates that the notes should be separated, as for a breath.

arpeggio		the wavy line indicates that the notes should be played from bottom to top in rapid succession.

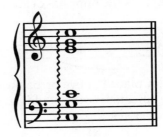

easured tremolo

a single slash above or below a note indicates a subdivision into eighth notes; a double slash indicates sixteenth notes; and a triple slash indicates either thirty-second notes or that the note(s) should be played as fast as possible.

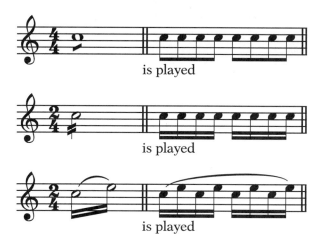

tr

the abbreviation *tr*, with or without a wavy line following it, indicates a rapid alternation with the diatonic second (or chromatic second if an accidental is included) above a written note. Performance practices and styles vary, but in general, seventeenth- and eighteenth-century trills begin on the diatonic step above and the modern trill begins with the note indicated.

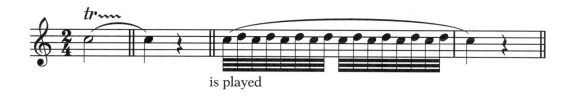

mata

indicates that a note should be held for longer than its normal value.

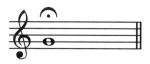